116754

Genesis

GENESIS
A Devotional Commentary
11673

Donald Grey Barnhouse

ZONDERVAN PUBLISHING HOUSE
Grand Rapids, Michigan

© 1970 by Zondervan Publishing House, Grand Rapids, Michigan

Congress Catalog Card Number 78-106434

Grateful acknowledgment is made to the Division of Christian Education of the National Council of Churches for permission to use many verses from the Revised Standard Version of the Bible © 1946 and 1952 by the Division of Christian Education of the National Council of Churches.

Printed in the United States of America

Foreword

This devotional exposition of Genesis was the crowning effort of a spiritual giant, Dr. Donald Grey Barnhouse. Midway in his progress verse-by-verse and phrase-by-phrase through Genesis he received his summons home and went to be with the Lord he loved so supremely and served so well. The wisdom and insight of his comments on these chapters will provide hours of profitable reading and worthwhile commentary for ministers and teachers of the Word.

In many instances Dr. Barnhouse uses his own literal translation of the verse or phrase being expounded, and in other instances he bases his comments on the King James Version of the Bible. He also makes extensive use of the Revised Standard Version of the Bible. His deep commitment to the inspired nature of the written Word of God is strikingly present in these rich interpretive comments on the early chapters of Genesis. It is a great privilege and pleasure for us to make these insight-filled comments available to Bible students of this generation.

THE PUBLISHERS

Contents

Genesis

Genesis 1

If our day does not start with the Lord, there can be no blessing. If it does start with Him, there can be nothing but blessing. His ways, like those of His wisdom, are ways of pleasantness, and all His paths are peace.

Verse 1: In the beginning God created the heaven and the earth

There are many beginnings described in the Word. This verse refers to the beginning of the material universe. The gospel of John goes back much farther into the eternity when there was not yet a material creation. A music teacher may tell a child to go back to the beginning, and it may be the beginning of a phrase, a measure, a page, a movement, a sonata. God is the God of new beginnings.

There is no peace for the mind apart from the knowledge that back of all that is around us, back of the stars and sun, the earth and all that is in it, back of our own bodies, fearfully and wonderfully made, there is the mind and will of God. When we know that He created all these things, we can know that He has an eternal purpose. Even though the universe is marked by the eroding signs of judgment upon sin, we can be sure that our God who began His work will also finish it. "When I begin, I shall also make an end" (I Samuel 3:12).

Verse 2. The earth was without form, and void

There is, of course, nothing that is "without form." The very fact of material existence predicates a shape to matter. It may be as fluid as a cloud, but there is form. The earth that became a wreck and a ruin was not made so in the beginning. Isaiah

9

uses the same Hebrew word to tell us that the Lord did not create the earth a wreck ("in vain," Isaiah 45:18).

The earth has always been a mirror of its inhabitants. When Lucifer was an unsinning cherub, the earth was perfect. When he fell, it became a wreck and a ruin. When Adam was created innocent, the world was a garden of Eden. When he fell, God cursed the ground for man's sake, and it became the mirror of fallen Adam.

Darkness was upon the face of the deep

A shroud is the garment of death. A corpse is wrapped to keep the horror of death from being too apparent. So God shrouded the world with the mantle of darkness. It did not hide the earth from Him, for the darkness and the light were both alike to Him (Psalm 139:12). Darkness is a phenomenon which demonstrates the insufficiency of the human eye. We know that light travels on wave lengths, and we can see nothing beyond red in one direction and violet in the other. The creatures of God's universe who followed Lucifer in his plunge to Satanhood were deprived of their heavenly vision, and the earth which had been the palace of their prince now was hidden from their eyes, as a testimony against sin.

The spirit of God moved upon the face of the waters

If God does not move, there can be nothing but death. The Hebrew word for "move" comes from a primitive root that means "to brood." It is beautifully translated elsewhere. "As an eagle stirreth up her nest, fluttereth over her young," so does the Lord move on behalf of His people. The word that is translated "moved" in Genesis is "flutter" in Deuteronomy 32:11. The heart may be an abyss of sin, but the Lord flutters over it, brooding with desire to have light penetrate it.

Verse 3: And God said, let there be light: and there was light

Modern physics has discovered that mass equals energy. Matter is power moving very fast. John tells us that "In the beginning was the Word. . . . " When we read, "And God said . . ." we have the going forth of the Word — Christ. Count the number of times in this first chapter of the Bible in which we read that "God said. . . ." That is the Word in action. That is why we read, "All things were made by him [Christ] and with-

10

out him was not anything made that was made" (John 1:3). "By the word of the Lord were the heavens made; and all the host of them by the breath of his mouth. . . . For he spoke, and it was done; he commanded, and it stood fast (Psalm 33:6, 9). God is sovereign. The absolute efficacy and finality of the outgoing Word is sufficient evidence for this divine sovereignty.

God had been able to see all the time. Now He let the universe see the earth as He saw it, in all the horrible deformity caused by sin. The impotence of any other will than His was made manifest. All that the light shone upon the first day was chaos.

Verse 4: And God saw the light, that it was good

In the early days of the race men went to sleep at nightfall and arose with the dawn. The mark of modern civilization is its artificial light.

There can be no question that most crimes are committed in the darkness, and sinful lusts take their hold when the lights are put out. "He that doeth truth cometh to the light, that his deeds may be made manifest, that they are wrought in God (John 3:21). The reality of our salvation is demonstrated by our love of His light. We are called children of the light, and children of the day. We are not of the night or darkness (I Thessalonians 5:5).

Verses 11, 12, 21, 24, 25: After His kind

God is a God of order. All things that exist are in groups that are interrelated. The farther science advances, the more it is realized that all things are interconnected. Not only are the various orders of living things made according to their various minds, but even in inanimate nature there is amazing orderliness with infinite variety. Every snowflake that ever fell upon the earth has a similar mathematical design, but no two are ever alike. All the elements in the chemical table are interrelated in weight and atomic structure. The great universe swings in predictable fashion. The astronomers know that a solar eclipse will be visible at a certain time in a certain place. They will travel to that spot, and the eclipse occurs exactly on time.

Verse 22: And God blessed them

The lower orders of creation were blessed by God. A curse

11

came upon the original creation because of Satan's sin and the later curse because of man's sin, but in the beginning there was nothing to cause destruction and nothing to mar. The creation moved on its perfect way; the curse had not yet come. All was blessed by God. The Society for the Prevention of Cruelty to Animals came as a by-product of Christianity. Even in lands where religion will not permit the killing of a flea, the monstrous cruelty to beasts of burden is proverbial. God puts kindness into the heart when Christ comes in. "A righteous man regardeth the life of his beast: but the tender mercies of the wicked are cruel" (Proverbs 12:10).

And the day will come, at the return of the Lord, when animals will not devour each other, and poison will be removed from insects and reptiles. They shall neither hurt nor destroy any more, "for the earth shall be full of the knowledge of the Lord, as the waters cover the sea" (Isaiah 11:9).

Verse 26: Let us make man in our image, after our likeness

It was not a physical image, for God is Spirit (John 4:24), and a spirit hath not flesh and bones (Luke 24:39). The physical descriptions of God are figures to teach our childish hearts some of the realities of His great love. No one knows the exact area or the full meaning of this image and likeness. I believe it refers to the trinity of our nature. A tree has a body, but no soul or spirit; an animal has a body and a soul (the Hebrew definitely uses the word for animals), and thus the foxes have their holes and the birds their nests; but man has spirit in addition to the soul and body.

This is a moral likeness — "righteousness and true holiness" (Ephesians 4:24), and an intellectual likeness — "renewed in knowledge after the image" (Colossians 3:10). It was lost in the fall and is regained in the new birth (I Corinthians 15:49). And finally "we shall be like him" (I John 3:2).

Let them have dominion

The word "dominion" means lordship, and comes from the same word we use for Lord when we write our year as *Anno Domini*. When man departs from God, the order is reversed and things have dominion over the man. In India the cattle have the dominion because they are worshiped. Thus the land has reached the abyss of degradation.. The Lord made man to be master of his environment, no matter what it is. Sin reversed this, but redemption restored it. In the Lord there is lordship.

Verse 28: Be fruitful

There is nothing more pitiful than an orchard that has had leaves and blossoms but which produces no fruit. The command in Genesis was for mankind to be fruitful in the production of children, but the spiritual meaning is carried over into the Word where the believer is set forth as being "fruitful in every good work" (Colossians 1:10). This fruitfulness is coupled with walking worthy of the Lord unto all pleasing, and even the fruitfulness has further fruitfulness, since the fruitful believer increases in the knowledge of God. The secret of fruitfulness is abiding in Christ, and there are four degrees set forth in Christ's sermon on the vine and the fruit. We are to have fruit (John 15:2), more fruit (v. 2), much fruit (vss. 5, 8), and fruit that remains (v. 16).

Verse 31: And God saw every thing that He had made, and, behold, it was very good

He hath done all things well (Mark 7:37). God couldn't create anything that was bad. Badness comes from the heart of Satan and from the heart of man. The law of sin and death that works in the world was created by God because of the sin, but the judgment is just as good as anything else that God ever made. It is good that material things should disintegrate, that worms should eat roses and that our sins should produce sorrow. These are the tender thoughts of God to teach His ways. It is as true today as it ever was that everything that God does is good and everything that any other will performs is marked by the death that is opposition to His true and perfect will.

Genesis 2

Verse 2: He rested on the seventh day

But not for long. As soon as man sinned God went to work again. The Lord Jesus Christ said, "My Father is working still, and I am working" (John 5:17, RSV). Since sin entered there has been no real rest for God or man. In another sense, of course, there is perfect rest in the Lord, and salvation comes to those who cease from their works as God did from His (Hebrews 4:10). The poor struggling soul who is ever seeking to do, do, do something for salvation has no peace at all. But those who labor to enter into His rest find the peace which passes all understanding (Philippians 4:7).

Verse 7: And the Lord God formed man of the dust of the ground

Even though we are fearfully and wonderfully made (Psalm 139:14), the glory is all the Lord's, and we have nothing whereof to boast. So low is dust that God gave it to the serpent for the food of his curse. Job uses the word twenty times to describe the littleness of man in his misery. It is to dust that all bodies return in death.

But we can look up to the Lord in confidence because "he knows our frame and he remembers that we are dust" (Psalm 103:14 RSV). This is a promise to believers; there is no word that the Lord remembers that the unsaved are dust. Dust that exalts itself is hateful, but dust that acknowledges its dustiness finds favor in the sight of the Lord.

And God breathed into his nostrils the breath of life

14

The dust was but dust until God touched it and put life into it by His Spirit. Breathe as deeply as you can. Hold it. You can't hold it much longer. There it goes. Try it again. Can you take a second nose-full before you breathe out the first? No. God uses that puny lack to call us away from ourselves. In the last verse of the second chapter of Isaiah the Hebrew might well be translated, "Cease ye from man who can only hold one noseful of breath at a time. What is he anyhow?" It is a breath that is corrupt (Job 17:1). But the breath of God gives frost (Job 37:10) and kindles Hell (Isaiah 30:33). The breath of God made the heavens (Psalm 33:6) and discovered the foundations of the world (Psalm 18:15).

And man became a living soul

The significance of man's original constitution is seen only when he is contrasted with the Lord Jesus Christ. The great resurrection chapter quotes this text and enlarges on it: "The first man Adam became a living being; the last Adam [Christ] became a lifegiving spirit" (I Corinthians 15:45 RSV). Man lives by inhaling; Christ gives life by exhaling. We are creatures; He is the Creator.

In this life the center of our being is the soul, but in the eternal life, which we possess from the moment of the new birth, the center of life should be in the renewed spirit, and will be in the spirit in the resurrection. For the body that is buried is dominated by the soul, but the body that is raised is dominated by the spirit (I Corinthians 15:44 Gk). Christians can wheeze along on the one-lung power of the soul, or can live the abundant life of the power of the risen Christ through the Holy Spirit.

Verse 9: The tree of life . . . in the midst of the garden

We do not know the nature of this tree, but we know that what man lost by sin, we have regained through the Lord Jesus Christ. On Calvary's hill another tree was raised, and the soul of Christ was poured out to pay the fine that the justice of God was forced to demand of us. When we make His soul an offering for sin, He gives us life eternal (Isaiah 53:10). Here is the tree of life, the cross of the Lord Jesus Christ. There is no blessing that can come to man apart from that which the Lord did for us there.

Verse 17: The tree of knowledge of good and evil

We do not know the nature of this tree, but we know that it was a symbol of man's dependence upon God. It was not any of the things that men have foolishly described it to be. It was not sex, since God had told men to multiply. It was not wine, since there was not yet sin, and therefore no curse, and no fermentation. Whatever it was, it was forbidden, and was the only limitation on man. It was the catalyst that brought man's will to its dreadful decision. He wanted his own way instead of God's way. Wanting one's own way is the worst of all sins, since it means abandoning God's way.

Thou shalt surely die

The death of the body is the separation of soul and spirit from the body. The death of soul and spirit is their separation from God. This is the death that Adam died, and in Adam we died also. It is in consequence of this death that we are born separated from God, estranged, aliens, godless, hopeless, Christless (Ephesians 2:12). The Hebrew reads, "In the day that thou eatest thereof, dying thou shalt die." It was to be a death that was absolutely sure from God's viewpoint, but man, though he is dead, still has a semblance of life.

The death we died in Adam is overcome only by the death of the Lord, for through death He destroyed Satan who had the power of death (Hebrews 2:14). By passing through Adam's death, we received death. By passing through Christ's death, we receive life.

Verse 18: It is not good that the man should be alone

God can be alone, for in Him are all the attributes of perfection. He is in three persons, and so was never alone in one sense. There was always the Father, who is love, the Son, who is the object of that love, and the Spirit of love between them. But man is a creature and cannot stand by himself. God, in His love, thought up the wonderful idea of home — of man and woman together, one flesh, and one mind and heart.

God created the home as the perfect triangle — the man, the woman and the Lord, and a threefold cord is not quickly broken (Ecclesiastes 4:12). As long as the Lord is on His point of the triangle, the edifice is sure. Then home life is to be centered on the Lord, as each encourages and prays for the other.

16

A helpmeet

The Hebrew conveys the idea of a helper *as before him,* even as your face in the mirror is before you. The woman was meant to be a helper suited to man's needs. The literal meaning of "counterpart" would express the idea. It was absurd to put two words together to form the etymological monstrosity *helpmeet.* This was done in the seventeenth century through ignorance and became widespread in the nineteenth century. The true idea of the woman is that she should be man's complement, to fill up that which is lacking in him. The woman should answer in every part to the need of the man, if she is to be a help fitting (not a helpfitting) to his life.

Verse 21: The Lord God . . . took one of his ribs

Here is the foundation of the union between one man and one woman. God did not make the woman out of the dust of the ground as He had made the man. The man had life, and God made the woman out of the live man. She was taken from under his arm that he might protect her and from next to his heart that he might love her.

We can understand this better when we dig under the English translation of Malachi 2:14, 15. "The wife of thy youth . . . thy companion, and the wife of thy covenant. And why made he only one wife? Was it because he did not have breath enough? Why did he make but one? That he might seek a godly seed. Therefore take heed to your spirit, and let none deal treacherously against the wife of his youth."

The Lord God caused a deep sleep to fall upon Adam

A deeper sleep fell upon the Lord Jesus Christ. Marriage is said to be an illustration of the relationship between Christ and the Church (Ephesians 5:32). The Lord came to earth and took a body of Adam's line through His mother. He came seeking His bride. It was only by the deep sleep of death that He could win her for heaven. The Father received His spirit in death. Then the soldier came and thrust a spear into the side of the Lord. Out of that wound in His side, came the Church which He purchased with His own blood (Acts 20:28). By that death we become bone of His bone and flesh of His flesh, and shall be His forevermore.

Genesis 3

Verse 1: He said, hath God said?

Here is the first interrogation point in the Bible. It follows a question on the lips of Satan. There would never have been any need for a question, if sin had not come. The first question was intended to cast doubt upon the Word of God. God had said, but Satan asks if God had really spoken. Here is the first denial of divine revelation and divine inspiration.

Verse 4: Thou shalt not die

God says, "Thou shalt surely die" (2:17). Satan says that God's Word is not true. The wreckage of earth and a million billion graves attest that God is true and Satan is the liar. He still clings to his lie, however. It comes today in various forms. He denies the eternity of the lake of fire. He teaches the doctrines of soul-sleeping and annihilation. He preaches the doctrine of a second chance of salvation after death.

Over against this, Christ said, "You will die in your sins unless you believe that I am he . . ." "You will . . . die in your sin; where I am going, you cannot come" (John 8:24, 21 RSV). The choice today is the same as it was for Eve — the Word of God or the denial of Satan.

Verse 5: Your eyes shall be opened

Their eyes were to be opened to earth but closed to heaven. They would be able to see sin, but they could no longer look on righteousness. Lust would attract them and holiness would blind them. They would know good and evil, but they would no longer have the power to choose the good, and they could no

18

longer resist the evil. They would aspire to be gods, but would fall into the pit of the demons.

"The god of this world has blinded the minds of the unbelievers, to keep them from seeing the light of the gospel of the glory of Christ, who is the likeness of God" (II Corinthians 4:4, RSV). But on the day of resurrection, the Lord Jesus Christ joined Himself to His disciples on the road to Emmaus, and as He brake bread in their house, "Their eyes were opened" (Luke 24:31).

Verse 6: Pleasant to the eyes

The woman was walking by sight and not by faith. God had said that they were not to eat of the fruit; that should have been enough. We may not understand why the Lord gives some of His commands, but to the child of trust it is enough that He has spoken. Satan and the flesh will present a thousand reasons to show how good it would be to disobey His command.

The only safe course is to trust implicitly in what He has said, and not to lean on our own common sense (Proverbs 3:5). There is no fear of God before the eyes of the wicked (Psalm 36:1). "The commandment of the Lord is pure, enlightening the eyes" (Psalm 19:8). It is only when our eyes are opened to behold wondrous things out of His law (Psalm 119:18) that we can see to walk by faith.

Verse 7: They knew that they were naked

It was not skin nakedness that they discovered, but the nakedness of their dead souls. It is more than probable that they were clothed in light before the fall, and when they sinned the light went out.

Light is the symbol of righteousness and both are mentioned in the Scriptures as a garment. God clothed Himself with light, as with a garment (Psalm 104:2). In the transfiguration, Christ's raiment was white as the light (Matthew 17:2).

When sin came there was nothing left of righteousness and they were naked indeed. We must not think of this as a change from blissful innocence of nakedness to a conscious knowledge of it, but from glory to nudity.

They sewed fig leaves together

Any port in a storm. They became aware of their condition

and they sought to cover themselves as quickly as possible. It was yet a long way down the hill of rebellion to the depravity of savages who go naked without shame. Fig leaves were a substitute for righteousness. "We have all become like one who is unclean, and all our righteous deeds are like a polluted garment" (Isaiah 64:6, RSV).

Verse 8: They heard the voice of the Lord God

What more wonderful sound! And yet they were terrified. Sin separates. Here we see the pursuing love of God. He would not leave them in their misery and nakedness. He would speak to them. But when man is running away from God the voice of tenderness takes on tones of awe. "The voice of the Lord is upon the waters . . . is powerful . . . is full of majesty . . . The voice of the Lord breaketh the cedars . . . divideth the flames of fire . . . shaketh the wilderness . . . maketh the hinds to calve . . . discovereth the forests" (Psalm 29). "He uttered his voice, the earth melted" (Psalm 46:6). That is the way the voice of the Lord must have come to their fleeing hearts, in spite of the fact that all the tones of tenderness and mercy were there.

Adam and his wife hid themselves

And, worst of all, they hid themselves from the presence of the Lord. This is the worst of all sins. A sin against one's own heart and life is bad, very bad. A sin that involves the soul of another is worse, much worse. But a sin that is an affront against the majesty and holiness of God is worst of all.

That is why David, after he had committed such a series of sins — adultery, murder — and had betrayed his kingship by failing to lead the people and by sending his subjects to their death in battle — cried out, "Against thee, thee only, have I sinned" (Psalm 51:4).

It was, of course, futile to attempt to hide from God, but sin will try any folly. "If I make my bed in hell, behold, thou art there!" (Psalm 139:8).

Verse 9: Where art thou?

God first called man when man was running away, and the Lord has been calling man ever since. "The Son of man has come to seek and to save that which was lost" (Luke 19:10). Man

20

runs away from God and thinks he has outdistanced Him. He turns back to look upon his path and then hears the Lord at his other side saying, "My child, I came by a shortcut to wait for you here."

The fleeing sinner can never escape the pursuit of love. Shall He who made man's feet not catch up with him? He calls the sinner to come to salvation and He calls the believer to worship in Spirit and in truth. "The Father seeketh such to worship him" (John 4:23).

Verse 10: I was afraid . . . and I hid myself

How far sin had carried man in the fall may be seen by this. The sinner who once loved to meet the Father in the cool of the day is afraid and hides himself when sin comes in to separate them. Nothing in this world separates like sin. And the separation is all on man's part.

The poet has well shown this when he sings

> O may no earthborn cloud arise
> To hide Thee from Thy servant's eyes.

The clouds do not come from heaven; they arise as the perspiration of the earth. Above them is the clear view through all of space to the heavens.

If man sins and runs away he wraps clouds around himself. They will not keep God from seeing him, but will keep him from seeing God.

Verse 11: Who told thee that thou wast naked?

The birth of conscience followed the entrance of sin. Satan had promised them that they would be as gods, knowing good and evil. But now they know the evil, and the sense of it arises out of man's own lost estate. Because of the truth of God written on the conscience God says, "Therefore you have no excuse, O man" (Romans 2:1, RSV).

Out of men's own hearts arises the witness that God is true, and that they have forsaken Him by nature. Men have within them that which has the power to tell them that they are naked, but which does not have the power to clothe them. But when the voice of God calls, and when He stirs up the conscience, it is because He wishes to arouse men to the sense of their need so that they will turn to Him. God never plows a field that He does not intend to plant.

21

Verse 12: The woman whom thou gavest to be with me

How low sin brought man is revealed in his first excuse. He is willing to hide behind the tenderest gift of God and to throw blame from his own shoulders to those of the weaker vessel. Adam's sin was far worse than that of Eve for she thought she was doing the right thing — she was improving the lot of her husband by yielding.

But man sinned in willful rebellion (I Timothy 2:14). She had been given as a help, fit for him. She was the channel but not the cause of his fall. Emphasize the word *Thou,* and you will see the heart of Adam's accusation. It is not against Eve; it is against God. "If you had created another type of wife for me, I . . ." But it was a lie.

Verse 13: What is this that thou hast done?

God does not discuss with Adam his flimsy excuse, but He now demands an accounting of the woman. She is in the fall as much as the man. Sin in ignorance is nevertheless sin. Her shame is as great as that of Adam. He sought to blame her and God, she seeks to blame the serpent. The fall brought with it what is now an instinct to get out from under the blame. But there is no place for man to hide except where God has provided a hiding place. "The hail shall sweep away the refuge of lies" (Isaiah 28:17).

Verse 14: Dust shalt thou eat

The serpent, which had evidently been upright in posture, and with the gift of human speech, suddenly hears the doom of judgment. Because it had been the channel of Satan's offices, it became a loathsome, crawling reptile. God was, of course, speaking also to Satan through the serpent, as the next verse shows, and this is why dust is the serpent's meat and shall be, even in the restored kingdom (Isaiah 65:25).

To eat dust is to know defeat, and that is God's prophetic judgment upon the enemy. He will always reach for his desires and fall just short of them. There will be continuous aspiration, but never any attainment.

Verse 15: I will put enmity between thee and the woman

God created the hatred that exists between Satan and humanity. It is a good thing, for were we to become friends and followers of Satan, there would be some victory for him. But he does not want the good of the race nor does the race want his good. Each, in fact, selfishly desires his own good. Therefore, there can be no community of interest to bring a coalition between man and Satan. A few may become the children of the devil, but the majority are incurably addicted to the love of their own interests. This is one reason why Satan can never triumph.

Her seed

Here is the first definite mention of the Lord Jesus Christ in His character as the Saviour of mankind. On the first pages of the Book we thus find the announcement of His coming and a foreshadowing of the fact that He was to be the seed of the woman. Here is the first teaching of the doctrine of the Virgin Birth of our Lord.

The word "seed" is found many times in the book of Genesis and is one of the keys to the book. In the New Testament the Holy Spirit tells us that the word is the singular because it refers to the Lord Jesus Christ (Galatians 3:16). The hatred that would be directed against the woman would also be directed against her greatest Son, the Lord Jesus. The highway of the cross begins here.

It shall bruise thy head

The power of Satan is to be crushed. He may rage for centuries, but his doom is sure. The Lord God has promised to make an end of him and will even bruise him under our feet shortly (Romans 16:20). When our Lord hung on the cross He not only provided redemption for sinners and vindication for the Lord God of Hosts, but He also accomplished the defeat of Satan.

The cross made a show of him openly, and the Lord triumphed over Satan in the hour of death, since by the cross he was overcome entirely (Colossians 2:14, 15). The prophecy was made, and at the cross the groundwork of its execution was manifest. It is just a question of time now, waiting for God's moment to bring all to fulfillment.

Thou shalt bruise his heel

Here is set forth the death of the Lord Jesus Christ. We do not know whether Adam and Eve had any real knowledge of the

23

fact that the feet of the Saviour would be pressed, literally, against the cross. But where Satan bruised Him physically, the Lord God did the mightier bruising, for "It was the will of the Lord to bruise him; he has put him to grief" (Isaiah 53:10, RSV). The Father put the Son to death, and there is the certain ground of our justification. In crushing Satan the Lord was crushed. In bringing death to the enemy, He Himself died. The enemy remains crushed, but the Lord rises from the dead.

Verse 16: I will greatly multiply thy sorrow

The lot of woman has been hard over the history of humanity. It is commonly said that this is a man's world. In no small sense it is, and the reason is to be found in the special curse that was put upon womankind at the time of the fall.

It is difficult for women in Christian lands to realize the miseries of their hundreds of millions of sisters in pagan lands, where the lot of woman is little above that of cattle. Where the Gospel has gone, the load has been lifted, and woman in Christ has become the reflection of the redeemed Church, the bride of Christ. Even the unsaved women in the lands that have a dominant Christian influence have profited by the ideals of freedom which the Gospel has brought.

Thy desire shall be to thy husband

It is inherent in the nature of woman to have but one great love in her life. If she is willing to live in that sphere, God can give her a joyful life. At the risk of stirring rebellion, I point out that most marriages in the world are made for women by their parents, and that love is expected to develop after marriage.

This is almost universally true in Asia and Africa, and it is a debatable question that the "freedom" of women in the western world is not responsible for the divorce evil and much of the breakdown of home life. This verse will be understood better when it is realized that the desire of man toward his wife alone is solely by God's grace and not by nature.

He shall rule over thee

This does not give man a servant when he marries, but a companion in Christ. In the pagan world the wife is a servant; in the Christian world outside of Christ the wife is frequently a rebel; in the world that is in Christ the true relationship of the home can be established.

The husband must always realize that in placing him as head of the home, God conferred upon him a high responsibility and an inestimable privilege. He is the high priest of the home and responsible for the family worship and for the spiritual tone of his house. God will hold every man accountable for this at the judgment bar. The rule is the tender one of love, and no woman will ever have any difficulty being in subjection to a man who is willing to be crucified for her (Ephesians 5:22, 25).

Verse 17: Because thou hast hearkened unto the voice of thy wife

Advice carries with it the consequences of responsibility. Adam sinned with calculated deliberation, knowing what he was doing (I Timothy 2:14). The result was a curse which exists to this day upon the very ground.

David met a woman and followed her advice and was blessed of the Lord because of it. When Abigail spoke to him, David replied, "Blessed be the Lord God of Israel, which sent thee this day to meet me; And blessed be thy advice, and blessed be thou . . . ." (I Samuel 25:32, 33). It was not the woman then, but her advice.

Cursed is the ground for thy sake

It would have been terrible if man had sat down in a pleasant world with nothing to occupy him. The only value of leisure is that it strengthens us for hard work. People who have nothing but leisure are parasites on society. A hard and resistant nature, warring against the labor of man, can teach man the nature of his own being: weeds grow more easily than crops, land must be cared for to prevent erosion; provision must be made against the future.

Verse 18: Thorns also and thistles shall it bring forth to thee

The thorns and thistles are not brought forth without purpose. They are not born to grow unseen and waste their sharpness on the desert air. They are brought forth *unto man*. God put every thorn on the earth to remind man of sin. The thistle is a sentinel of warning. Olives and grapes must be cultivated, and they will produce oil and wine, but thorn juice and thistle milk will nourish no man, and will bring no gladness to the countenance and no joy to the heart.

Men would build temples to false gods and God would ruin them and bring thorns and thistles upon them (Hosea 10:8). Instead of the thorn will grow the fir tree, and the myrtle will replace the brier (Isaiah 55:13). And the change comes because thorns pierced the brow of the Saviour (Matthew 27:29).

Verse 19: In the sweat of thy face shalt thou eat bread

Man was to know toil and fatigue. He was to enter into the struggle for existence, and in his labor he would long for the end of the day. This would teach him to long for the end of the day of sin, and to long for salvation that he might enter into the rest of God (Hebrews 4:3). But has he learned the lesson? How low sin has brought him, how true God's warning that eating the fruit would bring death is shown by the fact that we must change the above sentence to read: This *should* teach him to long for the end of the day of sin, and to long for salvation that he might enter into the rest of God. But man does not do what he should do, even if it is for his own good. Self-will has made each drop of sweat a distorting mirror.

Dust thou art, and unto dust shalt thou return

The first man had a low origin and sin brought him to a low destiny. This speaks of the body, for

> Dust thou art, to dust returnest
> Was not spoken of the soul.*

Man would live to see the soul and spirit move out of the body of a loved one and be left with cold clay. He would kiss the brow of the loved one and be chilled to the heart. He would be reminded by this greatest of all reminders that sin means death.

This lesson God had to teach the race in order to teach the greater lesson that sin's effects could be destroyed by the death of the Saviour.

Verse 20: Eve, because she was the mother of all living

As a matter of fact she was not the mother of anyone. There had been no birth before the fall, nor had there been conception. This is shown in the first verse of the next chapter. Moreover, Eve was not the name which God gave the woman. He saw her

*Henry W. Longfellow, *Psalm of Life*, Stanza 2

as a part of Adam and called her by her husband's name (Genesis 5:2). Eve is not a name, it is a title. It means "mother."

Adam was walking by faith. He had heard God say that the seed of the woman would bruise the serpent's head, and he believed that their only hope lay in a child. By faith he called his companion "mother," in the hope of promise.

Verse 21: Unto Adam also and to his wife did the Lord God make coats of skins, and He clothed them

This is the third garment worn by man in this chapter. He had been clothed in light and lost it by sin. He had made fig leaf substitutes and had been found naked. Now for the first time, blood was shed, and it was shed by God Himself. To use the skins of animals, it was necessary to slay them. This God did, and it would be difficult to find a simpler object lesson to show us that it would take the death of the Saviour, the Son of God, to clothe us with a righteousness which is not our own, but which comes from Him by virtue of His atoning death.

Verse 22: The man has become like one of us

The likeness was certainly not to that of any of God's wonderful attributes. It was merely that man now knew a great fact that he had not known before. He did not know that fact perfectly, and it would take the race thousands of years to learn the folly of it, but man now knew the difference between good and evil.

Long after, God said of them, "For my people are foolish, they know me not; they are stupid children, they have no understanding. They are skilled in doing evil, but how to do good they know not" (Jeremiah 4:22, RSV). If a man stepped off an airplane wing at 20,000 feet without a parachute, he would be up in the air like the pilot who could say, "That man has become as one of us, to know altitude and gravity." But there would be no power to maintain altitude or to avoid gravity.

Lest he . . . take also of the tree of life . . . and live for ever

How kind God was to prevent man from laying hold on something that would have kept him forever in his lost condition of death! How terrible it would be to live forever as we are now! The only thing that makes life bearable is the fact that it will end. God came in Christ and established another tree of life through death, and through that death, He destroyed him that had the power of death, the devil (Hebrews 2:14).

Verse 23: The Lord God sent him forth from the garden of Eden

It had now been demonstrated that environment could do nothing for man. There are those who think that the ills of our day are caused by the bad environment of children in the slums, or in some other place where circumstances are not just what the theorists desire. But environment can change nothing. Tie ribbons around a well-washed piglet, put him in a parlor and see which will change first, the pig or the parlor.

Verse 24: He drove out the man

It would seem that the man wanted to remain in the place of pleasant surroundings rather than walk in the will of God. God knew that the way up is down, but man had not learned that lesson. The history of the human race would scarcely suffice to teach that truth. "Every one who exalts himself will be humbled, and he who humbles himself will be exalted" (Luke 14:11, RSV).

How often it is necessary for God to drive us out of an apparent good to bring us to the place of real good! Abraham ran to Egypt instead of staying in the land of promise. Death forced Ruth to her salvation and motherhood in the line of the Messiah. In giving up Lazarus, Mary and Martha received Lazarus and Christ.

Cherubims, and a flaming sword . . . to keep the way

When I was a small boy I got the idea from a picture in a Sunday school leaflet that the sword was pointed against Adam who was thus kept from sneaking back. When I learned the Scripture, I realized that the cherubim were the supports of God's glory and majesty (Ezekiel 9, 10). Any angel of the lowest rank could have dealt with Adam. The flaming sword was pointed against Satan to keep him from destroying the way of access to the altar, which God had set up.

Before World War II President Roosevelt armed merchant ships, saying that we were "determined to keep the way to Iceland." This was to keep it open and free for our use. So the cherubim worked in behalf of Adam that he might have access to the altar, perhaps where God had provided the coats of skins.

The way of the tree of life

It was this scene at the gate of Eden, which at the command of God was reproduced by Moses on top of the ark (Exodus 25:18-22). The two cherubim, facing each other, bent over the place where the shed blood was placed by the high priest, once a year, on the day of atonement. God said, "There I will meet with you and from above the mercy seat, from between the two cherubim . . . I will speak with you." It was for this reason that David addresses God as "thou that dwellest between the cherubim" (Psalm 80:1). As soon as man sinned, God found him, and provided him a Saviour. He opened a way back to Himself and guards that way jealously lest anyone should close it.

Genesis 4

Verse 1: I have gotten a man from the Lord

In Hebrew the true meaning is found. "I have gotten a man, even the deliverer." Eve had heard the promise concerning the seed of the woman (3:15) and had believed that her child would be the answer, and that they would soon be back in Eden. So she named the baby, "Here he is!" for that is the meaning of Cain — "acquisition." But the baby turned out to be a murderer. She was learning what spiritual death really meant. She wanted deliverance, and a deliverer of her own making, but there was no true desire for the Lord Himself.

Verse 3: In process of time

God is a God of order. The Hebrew says, "at the end of days." There is probably hidden in this word the arrangement of God for a special day of offerings. We know from Hebrews 11:4 that Abel's offering was "by faith," and therefore he was obeying God's command, so there must have been a day of atonement commanded by God. We must not see here the religious institution of a seventh-day Sabbath, for the Sabbath was never known until the time of Moses (Nehemiah 9:14).

Cain brought of the fruit of the ground

It is not that God despises fruit, but the blood must come first. If Cain had first brought a lamb and then had said, "Lord, I love Thee so much, I want to bring a basket of beautiful fruit in addition," God would have showered him with blessings. He attempted to have a religion of beauty without the recognitions of the holiness and justice of God. Later, God demanded the

30

fruit (Leviticus 19:24). But the blood must come first.

To deny this order is to go in the way of Cain (Jude 11), which begins with self-will in religion and ends in murder and hell. "There is a way which seems right to a man, but its end is the way of death" (Proverbs 14:12, RSV).

An offering unto the Lord

We are not to bring what seems best to us but what He desires. It is not enough to worship God in our own way, we must worship in His way. "Those who worship him *must* worship him in spirit and in truth" (John 4:24, RSV).

In the book of Leviticus, God outlined the plan of approach to Himself down to the minutest detail. He was teaching the object lesson that He must be considered and not our whims. For His way always points to Christ. And if a member of Adam's race is to approach God, he must come through the grace of God by the way God has prepared. In the Old Testament it was through the offerings which He prescribed, for in His mind they pictured Christ, the only Way.

Verse 4: Firstlings of his flock

The Hebrew contains a beautiful thought which might be translated, "Abel brought the firstlings, and the fattest ones too." He did not pick a scrawny, ill-favored beast, but brought first-born lambs and the finest. Nothing is too good for God, and He has a way of giving back double for anything we give to Him. To give up the undesirable, the unwanted, or the superfluous is not surrender. There must be true sacrifice.

The highway to the cross was now firmly established. Here the first lamb is seen, one lamb for one man. Later, at the Passover, there will be one lamb for one household (Exodus 12). Then, on the day of atonement there will be one sacrifice for the nation (Leviticus 16). Finally, it is Christ who takes way the sin of the world (John 1:29). The individual, the covenant family, the nation, the world; all are in God's plan.

The Lord had respect

When I was a small boy, I saw an illustration of this text which showed two altars with the smoke of Abel's offering ascending toward heaven while the smoke of Cain's offering was blown toward the ground. If we are to follow the analogy

31

of the rest of the Bible, it was a divine fire that fell upon Abel's offering and consumed it.

Such a fire consumed the first of the tabernacle sacrifices (Leviticus 9:24); the sacrifice prepared by Gideon (Judges 6:21); that prepared by Elijah (I Kings 18:38); by David (I Chronicles 21:26); by Solomon (II Chronicles 7:1). It was a picture of the greatest fact concerning the death of Jesus Christ; namely, that God Himself put Him to grief (Isaiah 53:10). This is what gives value to the atonement.

Unto Abel and to his offering

God did not respect Abel because of what was in Abel, but because Abel believed God's Word about the blood sacrifice. Abel was as much of a sinner as Cain, but faith was counted to him for righteousness which he did not possess in himself. In the first pages of the Bible, the principle is established that the sinner and the sin-offering are bound together in the sight of God. We are bound up with Christ in His death.

Verse 5: Unto Cain and to his offering he had no respect

As the believer is bound up with Christ in the eyes of God, so the believer is bound up with the insulting substitute which he wishes God to accept instead of His only Son. We must not think of Cain as an iniquitous man at first, but as a cultured gentleman who thought that polished fruit was more esthetic than a blood sacrifice and who wished to consider the holiness of beauty rather than the beauty of holiness. I think of Cain when I see a man faultlessly attired walking on Fifth Avenue in the Easter parade after attending a church service where the bodily resurrection of Jesus Christ is denied.

Cain was very angry

The old nature becomes angriest when it is crossed. A man accused of losing his temper burst out, "But I never lost my temper once, if I got what I wanted." Wanting one's own way is the worst of sins because it is the first of sins. It leads to all others. "The mind that is set on the flesh is hostile to God" (Romans 8:7, RSV) simply because God and His interests stand as the barrier to self and its interests.

32

His countenance fell

The mouth speaks out of the abundance of the heart (Matthew 12:34) and the face reflects the thoughts of the heart. Every man's face is a history and a prophecy. The lines of sin are deeply etched, and the serenity of God is found in others. Both show what the man has been. I have seen a photograph of a man when he was living in sin and another photograph taken when that man had been indwelt by the Holy Spirit for several years, and he was, in deed as well as in principle, a new person.

The life lived under the domination of the Holy Spirit is still the best beauty treatment that this world can know. A face with that kind of beauty is a prophecy of heaven. It is not a beauty that is conformed to the Hollywood pattern, but a beauty that reveals the Lord.

Verse 6: The Lord said unto Cain

Oh, the marvelous condescension of the Lord that He should stoop to talk even for a moment with a sinner! For Cain was a murderer in his heart before he was a murderer with his hands. Why did not God reach out to destroy the sinner instead of coming to Him with loving pleading? The answer must be found in the nature of God. God is love. Even Cain was loved by God. Every spiritual child of Cain is loved by God.

Verse 7: If thou doest well, shalt thou not be accepted?

This does not mean that salvation was at any time on the basis of works; the whole Word cries out against any such interpretation. But the race was now being tested under the new knowledge of good and evil that had been received by the Fall, and it was about to be shown that such knowledge could not keep men from doing the evil or make them do the good.

"Conscience" can be divided into two parts, "con" meaning "with," and "science," meaning "knowledge." At times people say in parting, rather flippantly, "Let your conscience be your guide." But our guide must be the Word illuminated by the Holy Spirit.

If thou doest not well, sin lieth at the door

The love of God had provided what was necessary for bringing the sinner to Himself. Here the Hebrew word *chattath* which is translated "sin" is frequently found translated "sin offering." In Leviticus 4:3, for example, the word is used four times, and the context alone shows the difference between the sin that has been committed and the sin-offering that has been provided. To Cain God said, in effect, "If your conscience accuses you of sin, there is a sin offering crouching outside the door."

Unto thee shall be its desire

The Lord gave a submissive nature to the lamb that would cause the lamb to come to the foot of the man who would offer it up in sacrifice. There would be no fleeing lamb.

The amazing truth for the believer is that a holy Saviour is not offended by the approach of a guilty sinner. God the Father forsook Christ in the dark hour of the cross because holiness must fly from sin; but the Saviour's love could now be able to compass the sinner and draw even the lowest to Himself without defilement. Such is the value of the Saviour made sin for us. Such is the love of the Saviour that His desire is toward the child who puts his trust in Him. "For joy he endured the cross" (Hebrews 12:2); He was satisfied with His travail because of the believers (Isaiah 53:11).

Thou shalt rule over him

Historically, the promise to Cain was that if he would submit and turn to the sin offering, God would see to it that the lamb would be docile under his hand. But in type it is the glorious truth that the Lord in His love has provided Himself to be all for us. The lamb furnished wool for clothing, meat for food, and blood for atonement. Christ furnishes the righteousness for our garment, the bread for our soul's food, and the salvation from our sin.

Verse 8: Cain talked with Abel his brother

It is difficult to comprehend how much iniquity there is in our fallen hearts. Many are willing to admit that we all have certain evil tendencies but few are honest and sincere enough, or few have faith enough, to admit that this goes even to the roots of murder. Cain is a just picture of what we are by nature. Paul tells Titus that we live "in malice and envy, hated by men and hating one another" (Titus 3:3, RSV). Abel was unsuspecting so Cain approached him naturally and talked with him. We

34

do not know what he said, but it was designed to lure his brother to a lonely place and disarm his suspicions.

It was thus that Joab acted: He sent messengers after Abner, and took him aside . . . to speak with him privately (II Samuel 3:26, 27). Joab took Amasa by the beard to kiss him (II Samuel 20:9). Absalom made a feast to kill his brother (II Samuel 13).

Cain slew him

We look in vain for an extenuating motive. Envy and hatred are the only causes of this first murder. When God approved Abel's sacrifice, Cain should have looked into his own life to find out what was wrong. Instead, his envy led him to murder. "'Cain hated in him the divine image as much as he envied him the divine favor." The Holy Spirit takes the trouble to tell us that Cain slew Abel "because his own deeds were evil and his brother's righteous" (I John 3:12, RSV). Sin is always in the heart before it is in the deed. The death did not hurt Abel; there was the short, sharp pain of dying and then there was life for evermore. Cain thought to strike God through Abel; he really struck Abel through God, and Abel lived.

Verse 9: Where is Abel thy brother?

God's inquest is sometimes immediate and sometimes delayed, but every man will account for his deeds, the unsaved man before he goes to the lake of fire; the saved man at the judgment that will fix his rank and place in the eternal kingdom. Men grow bold because their divine arrest does not take place immediately following their sin. Their boldness turns to hardness because they seem to go unpunished. Their hardness leads to deeper sin and arrogance against God.

Am I my brother's keeper?

What folly sin brings! Did Cain come to the place where he thought that God could not see through the clouds or the darkness? Had he forgotten that perfect wisdom is a part of the Godhead? Sin produces the atheism of thinking that God is not here. Finally, when confronted by God, sin produces an arrogance of insolence and seeks to charge God with unrighteousness. It is as though Cain had said, "Can't you take care of your own world? Don't bother me about your creatures."

Men are the same today. If we accuse men of sin, they think

us unreasonable and first question the Word of God on which our accusations are based. When we affirm that God has spoken, they will not hesitate to deride His wisdom and righteousness.

Verse 10: The voice of thy brother's blood crieth

Cain thought he had stilled the voice of Abel so that there could be no witness against him. But Abel's blood had a voice that cried to God for ". . . he died, but through his faith he is still speaking" (Hebrews 11:4, RSV). "The life of the flesh is in the blood" (Leviticus 17:11).

Every sin has a voice which cries to God, and though there may be no human witnesses to it, the testimony of God will one day be given. On the cross the Lord Jesus cried, "My God, why hast thou forsaken me?" It took this cry to drown the voice of our sins which cried into the ears of God. Now, the Judge has become the Father, because the Saviour's blood paid the price, and the Saviour's voice quieted wrath against us.

Verse 11: And now art thou cursed

There are some men, cursed in Adam a first time, who are cursed from God a second time because of their own acts. The Lord Jesus Christ did something for every man, and everything for some men. The curse upon Adam was paid in full by the atoning death of our Lord who was made a curse for us, so that God does not hold Adam's sin against any man. Christ tasted death for every man (Hebrews 2:9); He is "the expiation for our sins, and not for ours only but also for the sins of the whole world" (I John 2:2, RSV); He is "the Saviour of all men, especially of those that believe" (I Timothy 4:10).

But every man has fallen a second time and his own deeds by willful choice have brought on the second curse. This, God will remove only from those who confess the Lord Jesus Christ as Saviour.

Verse 12: The ground . . . shall not henceforth yield unto thee her strength

In the first curse upon the ground, there was no mention of erosion or sterility of earth. Man would work and his work would produce adequate fruit. But now there is a second curse upon the land. Man would work and his work would be fruitless. The Lord enunciated the principle through Haggai: "Consider how you have fared. You have sown much, and harvested little; you eat, but you never have enough; you drink, but you never have your fill; you clothe yourselves, but no one is warm; and he who earns wages earns wages to put them into a bag with holes. Thus says the Lord of hosts: Consider how you have fared" (Haggai 1:5-7, RSV). The earth is always to reflect the spiritual nature of its inhabitants.

A fugitive and a vagabond

Cain was going to flee, but, of course, he could never get away from what was pursuing him because it was in his heart. When he was out of breath, he would merely wander. Then he would start running again. From henceforth every rock would hide an enemy, and in every shadow he would fear an avenger.

For the unsaved man there is no place to hide. Only for those who come to the Lord Jesus Christ can there be rest. All the life of the earthling is a barren search for something to allay fear and to ease the desperation of the flight. This is why men drink and scramble madly for wealth. It is even for this that men take recourse to religion without God — any port in a storm; any foxhole when the firing gets heavy.

Verse 13: My punishment is greater than I can bear

Not the faintest whisper of penitence; not the smallest sign of sorrow for sin; not the remotest desire for the grace of God. It is certain that Cain pitied himself as he fled and commiserated with himself in his wanderings. God, he thought, was indeed a hard God to give him such a lot.

One of the consequences of sin is that it makes the sinner pity himself instead of causing him to turn to God. One of the first signs of new life is that the individual takes sides with God against himself.

Verse 14: Every one that findeth me shall slay me

Not anyone, but everyone shall slay me. Cain was conscious that his sin merited wrath, but he only wanted to avoid the immediate and deserved consequences. Here was remorse but not repentance. Remorse comes from the Latin word which means to bite again; a morsel is a little bite. Sin does bite the sinner, and he uses any kind of opiate to stop the pain.

Repentance is godly sorrow. It means a right-about-face;

37

trusting the Lord once despised and rejected, and turning away from the self once trusted. Now self is despised and rejected and the Lord is the object of love and faith. Cain knew nothing of this. Thus does sin distort the vision and cause the further degradation of the sinner.

Verse 15: The Lord set a mark upon Cain

Whether the Hebrew word be translated "mark" in the sense of a brand or whether it be translated "sign" or "pledge" or "token" as in other passages, makes no real difference. The Lord was saying that at this time there should be no capital punishment. He changes this after the flood, but in this age where man has received the knowledge of good and evil, every man is responsible to that conscience.

God tests men in different ways at different times but every test yields the same result. Nothing in man can fulfill the demands of God's requirements. Cain was to live on and furnish yet an illustration of the truth of God's Word. Death was to be manifested in its foulest forms. What had begun in pride and self-will was to end in outer darkness.

Verse 16: Cain went out from the presence of the Lord

The presence of the Lord was the altar where the blood was shed. This place was protected by the cherubim with the flaming sword. It was the place where Abel had brought his lamb and where Cain, in blasphemy, had brought his fruit. He had been willing to recognize the God of providence in the harvest, but not the God of grace in the blood. Now his wickedness shows its last arrogance. He turns his back on the one possibility of redemption and goes his own way. God was present, of course, watching over Cain in all his wanderings, but Cain had left Calvary behind.

Cain . . . dwelt in the land of Nod

Adapting the work of one commentator, we see: Nod means "wandering" and the prophecy of Cain's vagabondage was now fulfilled (verse 12). He started with human reason as opposed to divine revelation; he continued in human willfulness instead of divine will; he opposed human pride to divine humility; he sank to human hatred instead of rising to divine love; he presented human excuses instead of seeking divine grace; he went into wandering instead of seeking to return; he ended in human loneliness instead of in divine fellowship. To be alone without God is the worst thing that earth can hold, to go thus into eternity is, indeed, the second death.

Verse 17: Cain knew his wife

How many unbelievers have used this woman as an excuse for their departure from the Word of God! Yet Genesis 5:4 says that Adam and Eve had daughters. And if it be argued that a man may not marry his sister, we answer that a stream is purer at the source than at the mouth.

Who would not prefer to drink from the Mississippi in upper Minnesota than at New Orleans? Every generation, like cities on the banks of a stream, puts its sewage into the human race. Adam married even closer than a sister; he married his own rib! Only a man who is looking for an excuse to get away from God will be troubled by such questions as this.

He built a city, and called the name of the city, after the name of his son, Enoch

Misery loves company, and in that fact is the beginning of urban civilization. Man seeks to surround himself with his fellows to fortify himself against God. Cain was a vagabond even though he had settled down. He was a wanderer at heart even though he slept in the same bed for the rest of his life.

Of such as Cain the Psalmist wrote, "Their inward thought is, that their houses shall continue for ever, and their dwelling places to all generations; they call their lands after their own names" (Psalm 49:11). He calls his son's name Enoch, "dedication," and thus makes a profession of religion without any possession. As there was no hint of the knowledge of sin and the thought of redemption in his offering of fruit, so now there is no indication of repentance. He calls his son "dedication," but he has not given himself up.

Verse 18: And Methusael begat Lamech

In Scripture, names are always significant. God gives us no information about the third, fourth, fifth and sixth generations from Adam except that the grandson of Cain was Irad, "witness," and that the next two generations combined the name of

God, *El* with their names. There was a form of godliness but no power.

The whole civilization reached its flower in the seventh generation, and it would show what the line of Cain could produce in ungodliness. In Cain's line, Enoch is a fleshly dedication; Seth's line produces the Enoch who walks with God. In the godly line, Lamech, "humility," fathers Noah; but in the ungodly line, the Lamech, the seventh from Adam, is earthiness personified. "Humility" comes from *humus,* earth; and it is possible to have it mere dirt as in Cain's Lamech.

Verse 19: Lamech took . . . two wives . . . Adah . . . Zillah

Here is the beginning of polygamy on the earth. The lusts of the flesh have conquered the minds of men. Nature's order is turned upside down. The names of the women are Adah, "beauty," and Zillah, "adornment." Scripture teaches that God hates fleshly glamor. Of godly women, the Holy Spirit writes, "Whose adorning [lit. word] . . . let it be the hidden man of the heart . . . a meek and quiet spirit, which is in the sight of God of great price" (I Peter 3:3, 4).

There is more than a hint in our text of the rise of woman to a place contrary to that which God gave her (3:16), with her desire to her husband. A softness enters civilization as though to cushion the blows that had fallen on Cain and to quiet his wandering heart. But it was of no use.

Verses 21, 22: The harp and the organ . . . artificer in brass and iron

The arts are legitimate if they are enjoyed in the light of redemption and with a full recognition that they are transitory and contain temptation. The descendants of Cain, whose religion seeks to improve the fallen creature, went out from the presence of the Lord and sought to make the ruined world happy by building cities, producing music and works of art. Here is the attempt to make life easy, civilized and safe. It is rather safe to assume that Jubal played dances and not psalms, for God says of such, "In the pride of his countenance the wicked does not seek him; all his thoughts are, 'There is no God'" (Psalm 10:4, RSV).

Verses 23, 24: Lamech said unto his wives . . . hearken unto my speech

Lamech composed this ode, perhaps the first poetry of earth: "I have slain a young man who merely wounded me, a young man who merely hurt me. God may take care of Cain sevenfold, but I will take care of myself seventy-seven fold" (Hebrew). It was the height of blasphemous arrogance. The first murderer had produced a grandson who was a murderer. The first murder was committed in envy, this one in pride.

We may see Lamech strutting before his two wives, boasting of his bloody deed. The cup is almost full of wrath. And by noting that Lamech was the seventh from Adam, and that God calls Lamech's cousin Enoch seventh (Jude 14), we can realize the force of Enoch's testimony, using the word "ungodly" four times in as many lines (Jude 15). Lamech's was the hard speech of an ungodly sinner against God.

After this tremendous picture of a civilization of the arts, and the triumphant song of a murderer, then . . . silence. We never hear of Cain's line again. In the space between verses 24 and 25, we must see the rising waters of the flood and hear the shrieks of these people as they were carried off to their doom.

It is interesting to note that God says of every son of Seth "and he died," except Enoch, whom He took alive to heaven. Of Cain's line there is no mention of death. The reason is that they were dead already. Of the woman who lives in pleasure, God says she is "dead even while she lives" (I Timothy 5:6). It was true of the men also. In the line of Seth, physical death is not separation from God, but triumph; but in the line of Cain, the second death has carried all its sons away to outer darkness. Physical death for them is anticlimax.

Verse 25: Seth, for God said she, hath appointed me another seed

It is impossible to destroy the plan of God. The prophecy at the judgment of the serpent was that the seed of the woman should bruise the serpent's head. Satan immediately made war on the idea, and in getting one son to kill his brother, he thought he had destroyed the possibility of fulfilling the promise.

But another son was born, and his name, Seth, means "appointed." He was chosen in Christ before the foundation of the world, and the line of the Saviour was now sure. It is interesting to note that Eve recognized that Seth was replacing Abel and not Cain. There was a glimmer of spiritual comprehension.

Verse 26: Then began men to call themselves by the name of the Lord

I prefer this marginal translation to that found in the King James or the RSV text. Exodus 6:3 tells us that men did not understand the name *jehovah* to be a name of God. It was jehovah with a small *j*, as we would speak of a saviour who saved our lives. God had promised a deliverer and men somehow called themselves by His name. Their comprehension was small but their faith was great. They were allying themselves to the Lord and were calling themselves His people.

Genesis 5

Verse 1: In the likeness of God made he him

This does not mean, of course, that God has a physical body. A tree has a body, an animal has a body and a soul (so the Hebrew states), and man has body, soul and spirit. We are a trinity. Our likeness to God is moral and intellectual. The likeness was lost in the fall and is regained in the new birth. The believer must always remember that God saved him in order that this likeness might be fully restored.

The purpose of predestination was that we might be conformed to the image of God's Son (Romans 8:29). The whole of the sculpturing, whittling, sandpapering process of the Christian life is to this end.

Verse 2: Blessed them, and called their name Adam

Eve is not a name, it is a title. God's name for the woman is Adam. She is looked upon in her husband. That is why Miss X when she marries Mr. Y becomes Mrs. Y. It is difficult to identify a woman apart from her husband. Who is she? Oh, her husband is Senator Smith. Who is she? Oh, she is the girl who married the garbage collector. Women are to lose their identity in the identity of the husband, because marriage is a picture of the church and Christ, and we lose our identity in Him.

Verse 3: In His own likeness, after His image

When Cain was born, Eve thought she had the little saviour, the little deliverer. But he was Cain, the murderer. Now Adam

43

and Eve have another son, Seth, and there is no more doubt. Seth and all the other sons of Adam are born after the likeness of Adam, and are in the image of Adam. There are no human beings on this earth in the image of God. To be in His image we must be born again (Ephesians 4:24; Colossians 3:10).

Verse 4: Sons and daughters

Supposed difficulties in the Bible fade when we read all of the Word of God. Some wonder where Cain got his wife, but the Bible shows us an ever increasing family.

Sidney Collett, in his book, *All About the Bible,* shows that if only a portion of the race married, and if only a portion of those had children, the population of the earth was at least a million by the time Adam died, 930 years after his creation. We believe that all grew up, and married and had large families. In all probability Adam saw five million of his own progeny on the earth before he died.

Verse 18: He begat Enoch

In the fourth chapter we find there is an Enoch who is the grandson of Adam through Cain. Now we find another Enoch who is one of the godliest men of the Bible. God does not want the two confused, so in the book of Jude he tells about Enoch, the seventh from Adam, not the third from Adam.

God is saying, "Do not get my Enoch mixed up with the devil's Enoch." God has an Enoch; the devil has an Enoch. God has convicts; the devil has convicts. God has millionaires; the devil has millionaires. God has doctors; the devil has doctors. God has preachers; the devil has preachers. "Do not get them mixed up," says God.

Verse 19: Jared lived after

In the whole line of Seth, Jared was the only one who outlived his son. But even though Enoch was not found when he disappeared, there must have been joy in the heart of Jared, for "a wise son makes a glad father" (Proverbs 10:1, RSV).

Since Jared, many parents have seen children go to be with the Lord; they sorrow not as others who have no hope. I know a family that has two children with them and two with the Lord. Their answer to the usual question about the number of their children is, "We have two in the land of the living and two with us in the land of the dying." There is no sting to death such as this.

Verse 21: Enoch begat Methuselah

The man who walked with God has a son with a strange name. Methuselah means: "When he is gone it will come." Strange? No. Enoch was troubled over the ungodliness of his cousins, and God's announced judgment. When would it come? Watch the little baby grow to be the oldest man ever to live on the earth. The name of the child was a revelation from God.

There is evidence that the soul of Enoch was greatly aroused because of the sin of his contemporaries, and the more evil the world became, the closer he walked with God. His godliness was written even on the name and life of his son.

Verses 22, 24: Enoch walked with God

Walking with God implies, first, agreement: Enoch had faith and was reconciled to God through the sacrifice. There could have been no agreement apart from this. Second, surrender: Enoch was surrendered to the will of God. He was a sinner like every other son of Adam, but he was a redeemed sinner, and was taking every advantage of his position. To walk with God is not an honor peculiar to Enoch; it is open to every man and woman who has received Christ. It means access to God at all times and coming with boldness into the holiest of all.

This was not a casual stroll. The walk of verse 22 is still going on in verse 24, three hundred years later. Jude tells us that Enoch preached. You can tell about his walk from the character of his preaching, for you discover that he used the word "ungodly" four times in five lines. The cousins among whom he lived were ungodly, and he had no reticence about labeling them as such.

To walk with God is to learn to call things by His vocabulary, and Enoch used the word "ungodly" for ungodly people. And he has this testimony that he pleased God (Hebrews 11:5). He may not have pleased his cousins, but he pleased God.

And he was not; for God took him

God tells us that Enoch did not see death (Hebrews 11:5). His family looked for him but "he was not found." That must have been a man hunt! God took Enoch to furnish the great type

45

of the translation of the Church at the end of this age. Every New Testament truth has its Old Testament type. The flood of judgment was to come upon the world even as the Great Tribulation is to come in the future. Enoch was taken out alive, even as those who shall not see death at the Lord's return.

Verse 27: Nine hundred and sixty-nine years

This is the record for longevity in the history of the human race. Methuselah's life is one of the greatest illustrations of the grace of God. The Lord had told Enoch to name the boy "When he is gone it will come." And as he grew older, and older, and yet older, it seemed as though God could hardly bring Himself to judge the world. As long as Methuselah lived, the door of God's patience was wide open. Likewise, God is stretching out the day of grace.

Verse 29: This same shall comfort us

The Lamech who named his son Noah, "comfort," was God's Lamech, quite different from the devil's Lamech (4:23) who committed murder and wrote poetry about it. God's Lamech seems to have been downhearted over the toil that was his lot as a member of the race of Adam. He may have been the first man to experience a crop failure, or to go through some adversity, but he lived in hope. Undoubtedly he heard the preaching of his grandfather, Enoch, and the promise of judgment connected with his own father's life. He called his son's name "comfort" as though he were still trusting in the promise that some seed of the woman would come to bruise the serpent's head.

Genesis 6

Verse 2: The sons of God

We believe that these sons of God were angelic beings, followers of Satan, who kept not their first estate, who left their own habitation, and who already have been placed in chains awaiting judgment (II Peter 2:4; Jude 6). This explanation complements the two New Testament passages and explains the flood and much that follows. It serves, also, to show the horror of sin, for ages of sin cannot change the nature of the being that is set against God. Only those beings, angelic or human, who are restrained by grace, can walk in the way of the Lord.

Verse 3: My spirit shall not always strive with man

Sin had been manifesting itself increasingly. The murder by Cain, the apostasy of his descendants, the bigamy of Lamech, and the ungodliness of all that line, were marks of what man is by himself. To these horrors was now added the irruption of demons upon the earth.

God could not beget the Messiah in the womb of a demon-possessed woman, and Satan was attempting nothing less than the degradation of the entire race. The Lord announces a definite term upon the rebellion — 120 years, and then judgment would come. It is remarkable to note that not one person repented. Here is the evidence that the Spirit, long resisted, will cease to strive with man.

An hundred and twenty years

The Lord, of course, knew that there would be but Noah and his family in all that one hundred and twenty years, yet He announced the season of grace and kept the way open till the last moment. The Christian witness must never grow tired of working without results. Evangelism is not soul-winning, but it is evangelizing. It is just as important that the Gospel should be preached to those who reject it as to the "few souls" (I Peter 3:20) who will be saved.

Verse 4: Giants . . .

The word is in our English translations because the Septuagint rendered the Hebrew by the Greek word for giants, but the original word portrays those creatures, half men, half demons, who were born of the horrible rebellion of the demons. These were "the mighty men that were of old, the men of renown." Here is the basis for the legends of Hercules and the other children of the gods of mythology.

The "after that" refers to the same phenomenon at the time of Abram's entry into Palestine. The devil had his brood there to await the arrival of Joshua. This was why all the people of the land were to be killed. God was not showing cruelty, but manifesting love in protecting His own by ordering the removal of these monsters.

Verse 5: The wickedness of man was great

God saw that the wickedness of man was great. This phrase refers to the actual doings of man. And it is the verdict of God. It is just as true of the earth today as it was of the period before the flood. Christ said, "As it was in the days of Noah . . . ."

The thoughts of His heart

Human eyes see the wickedness of human actions, but only God can tell what goes on in the hidden chambers of the heart. Here He tells us what He found. The hearts of men were evil; the thoughts of their hearts were evil; every imagination of the thoughts was evil; furthermore, this state was only evil, and it was not a temporary state, but was evil continually.

Who is capable of writing such a sentence? Only God, who has said, "I know the things that come into your mind" (Ezekiel 11:5, RSV), and who "weighs the spirit" (Proverbs 16:2).

Imagination

The word "image" is to be found in imagination, for it rep-

48

resents the pictures we allow to come to the eyes of our hearts. Throughout the Bible the imagination is an evil, accursed thing. It is urgently needful to wage war in this area, because the world feeds the imagination.

A four-year-old put on a Superman suit, jumped out the window, broke a leg, and was astonished that the suit did not protect him. A neurotic woman confessed that she lived in a dream world of romance. God says, "Casting down imaginations, and every high thing that exalteth itself against the knowledge of God, and bringing into captivity every thought to the obedience of Christ" (II Corinthians 10:5).

Verse 6: It repented the Lord

We must not suppose that God was astonished, or taken unaware. Elsewhere He has said, "The Glory of Israel will not lie or repent; for he is not a man, that he should repent" (I Samuel 15:29). If we do not believe that God has always known all things, we do not believe in God. This verse means that from the viewpoint of man it looks as though God were changing His mind, though He is really teaching that sin brings the display of His wrath.

It grieved Him at His heart

We are not to think that God's eternal joy and happiness in the knowledge of His perfections could be disturbed. God is not a disinterested watcher of the human scene. One of the marks of personality is feeling, and if God did not feel grief, He would be imperfect in His love.

Verse 7: I will destroy man

The terrible resolution which the Lord announced and executed was justly merited. From the beginning God had promised that the seed of the woman should bruise the serpent's head (3:15). The race was now largely demon-possessed and it was only right that man, woman and child should be destroyed. Justice and love could do no less.

Even if there had not been the satanic element, no one could criticize God for taking life when and as He wishes. He is the giver and maintainer of life, and He may do what He pleases when He pleases. On what grounds would God be told that He can bring death to millions of people at the end of a "normal" life span, but that He may not do it in any other way? God is just.

Verse 8: Noah found grace

There was no grace in Noah; the grace was in the eyes of the Lord. That is true of all God's dealings with man. Nothing in the sinner could appeal to God. Noah was no different from any other son of Adam. If the grace of God had not restrained him, the evil in his heart, which was just as great as the evil in the other hearts that were destroyed, would have manifested itself in a wickedness as great as theirs. In the eyes of God's justice all were to be seen as corrupt. But it pleased the Lord to look upon Noah in grace, simply because it pleased Him thus to look upon Him.

Verse 9: Noah was a just man

There was no justice in Noah. This means that Noah was a justified man. Through rose-colored glasses everything has a rosy hue. Through blue glasses everything looks blue. God looks at the sinner through Jesus Christ and he takes on the hue of the holiness of Christ.

God was looking at Noah through the Lord Jesus Christ, for he found grace in the eyes of the Lord. Grace can never be any place else. No man is just in the sight of God, for by the deeds of the law shall no flesh be justified in His sight (Romans 3:20). Noah had been quickened by God, and the new life within him believed God's Word about the blood. This was his justice.

And perfect in his generations

The word "perfect" does not mean that he had righteousness in himself, but that God was looking at him through Christ. He was accepted in the Beloved. His righteousness was the righteousness of God, placed to his account by grace. The life with which God had quickened him was in control of his being.

Noah walked with God

Noah and his great-grandfather, Enoch, are the two men before the flood who are said to have walked with God. Their lives show that it is possible to grow a lily in a manure pile. No circumstances of this world are too low for God to produce therein faith and holiness.

Our Lord said that "as it was in the days of Noah" so shall it be before His return. If those horrible days are to be repeated, every Christian should know that it is possible to walk with God in the midst of such unbelief and rebellion. No path can be so rough that a Christian may not walk safely, when he walks with God.

Verse 12: All flesh had corrupted his way

The worst of all sins, since it is the root of all other sins, is to desire one's own way. "All we like sheep have gone astray; we have turned every one to his own way" (Isaiah 53:6), is God's view of the departure of man. To turn to one's own way is to leave the will of God. The shortest definition of sin is: "I will," for it is the opposite of God's will.

In the beginning, the way of man may have seemed not far away from the way of God just as a line diverging from another straight line at a very small angle may seem close at first. But the evil of a life that is lived at a tangent from God is that it goes ever farther from God. Man's way ends in corruption.

Verse 13: God said unto Noah

The confidant of God receives from Him messages of joy and messages of despair. It is not easy to learn from God that one's whole world is to be destroyed and that one is to be committed to a strange barque and pass through an unprecedented flood. God is ever at work building the hearts of His children, and always leads them into the counsels of His own judgment after He has shown them the heart of His mercy.

Throughout the Bible we find God telling His choice ones the terrors of His judgment which He is about to pour upon the godless. "Surely the Lord God does nothing, without revealing his secret to his servants the prophets" (Amos 3:7, RSV).

I will destroy

The nature of God is justice to balance His love. The fact that God's time of patience will end and He will strike out in justice is the hope of the sin-cursed universe. If God does not act to destroy, then we face an eternity of sinfulness. But God is holy and just, and therefore He will destroy. For believers He has

51

already moved to destroy their sin by placing it on Christ and dealing with it for eternity, but upon those who will not enter into Christ, the flood of His wrath must fall. Hell is as much a part of the love story of God as heaven.

Verse 14: Make thee an ark

Here is a challenge to faith on an unprecedented scale. What would you do if God commanded you to build an 18,000-ton ship? When God commands the impossible, it is, of course, necessary that He supply the faith and the growth and the maturity of the faith. The work in the life of Noah was the greatest work that God did in this whole deluge episode.

Far more power was needed to fill the life of this "preacher of righteousness" to undertake this stupendous task than would be exercised in the destruction of the world. Spiritual power is always greater than physical power. One of the greatest acts of faith in the history of the world was when Noah stretched out his hand and grasped the first tool to build the Ark.

God Himself tells us in the New Testament that the Ark is a symbol of the Lord Jesus Christ, our Saviour (Hebrews 11:7). To Noah, building the Ark was a command, and he obeyed with joy. God commands all men to repent (Acts 17:30), to enter into the ark of safety before He pours out His eternal wrath upon all unbelief.

Pitch it . . . with pitch

The beauty of this passage is that the Hebrew word for "pitch" is the same as the word for "atonement." Leviticus 17:11 might read, "For the life of the flesh is in the blood; for I have given it to you upon the altar to be pitch for your souls, for it is the blood that serves as pitch for the soul."

There can be no leak in the Ark for it is the pitch that keeps the waters from entering. And the judgment of God can never touch the believer because the death of the Lord Jesus Christ stands between him and the wrath of God forever.

Verse 15: The length . . . the breadth . . . the height

A Christian engineer, lecturing before a War College meeting at Annapolis, said to the Admirals who are responsible for our navy that for centuries men built ships in various proportions. Since British naval architects had found the formula for the bat-

52

tleship *Dreadnaught,* all naval construction follows the proportions of that ship, now recognized as scientifically perfect. The proportions of the *Dreadnaught* were exactly those of the Ark!

Verse 16: A window . . . a door . . . lower, second and third stories

This verse means that there was an opening all the way around the Ark. Or God may have lighted the Ark with His presence even as He brought light to Israel when there was darkness in all Egypt. There was only one door to the Ark just as there is only one way to God. Inside, the believer is safe from all the floods of judgment. The fact that there were three decks speaks of the fact that there is room enough for all to come.

Verse 17: I do bring a flood

As for God, His way is perfect (II Samuel 22:31), and even His judgments are perfect. The most important doctrine in all the Bible is that of the sovereignty of God. None other can approach this doctrine in importance. Instead of criticizing God for sending the Flood, the criticism should be for saving Noah of the drunken heart and Ham with the foul and lustful mind. If they had received their just deserts, they would have been destroyed in the Flood. There is no mystery in the thought of judgment — the mystery is in the thought of grace.

Verse 18: My covenant

My promise, My terms of alliance, or rather My binding of Myself in grace. God has never acted by whim. All that He does is according to an eternal plan, set forth in various relationships with men by promises and covenants which are binding upon God. God says in the New Testament, "I use a simple human illustration: If it be but a man's covenant, one party cannot cancel or add to it" (Galatians 3:15).

Verse 19: Two of every sort

This is the God of creation ordaining the preservation of all the species of His creation. This is Elohim continuing His providential care over His creatures. Just as He created every living thing "after its kind" (Genesis 1:24, 25), so now He preserves every living thing "two of every sort."

The fact that He specified "male and female" is the accentuation of the idea of preservation. Not even a sparrow falls without His knowledge (Matthew 10:29), and every creature in His creation plays its part in His eternal plan.

Verse 22: Thus Noah did

Of all the men of the Bible it seems to me that Noah displayed the greatest faith. For we read in the New Testament that Noah obeyed the warning of God concerning things not seen as yet (Hebrews 11:7).

We must realize that it had never rained upon the earth. Rain was one of the things not seen as yet. What a fool Noah must have seemed to those who lived around him, when he warned of a change in nature that was one of the greatest in geological history. He did not waver. So, in a world where a mist went up and watered the earth (Genesis 2:6), Noah did exactly as he was told and built a ship of 18,000 tons' displacement.

All that God commanded him, so did he

Disobedience does not necessarily mean not doing what one is told to do. Disobedience may be total when one has done ninety per cent of what was commanded. True obedience consists not only in doing what one is told to do, but in doing *all* that one is told to do. So did Noah. Disobedience could have been as dangerous as building the ark without a floor, or with a hole in the floor. The water would have come through and the rest of the work would have been spoiled.

Genesis 7

Verse 1: And the Lord said unto Noah

Some allege that because a different name for God is used here that an editor took two different accounts and pasted parts together to form the present story. This is a total misconception of the spiritual. God *(Elohim)* is the creative name of the Godhead; Jehovah is the redemptive name. The previous verses speak of the preservation of the human race and the animal species. These verses speak of redemption. God who has acted in faithfulness to a promise now acts in utter grace. The two must go together.

For thee have I seen righteous before Me

What is beauty? Ask the critics, and after much discussion they will tell you that it depends on the person who does the looking. What is admired by one person is despised by another. This leads us to conclude that beauty is in the eye of the beholder. In ourselves there is no loveliness, but God has deigned to look upon us through the Lord Jesus Christ.

As a child may find a deformed toy lovely and precious because of something in the heart of the child, so the Lord found us righteous before Him because of something in His heart. And that something is what He has seen in Christ who is made unto us righteousness (I Corinthians 1:30).

Of every clean beast thou shalt take to thee by sevens

Here the critics cry, "contradiction!" because, they say, in the Elohim account God commanded two and in this, the Jehovah

55

account, God commands seven. But the explanation is found in the word "clean." Of all living things there were two for preservation of species. In addition, clean beasts by sevens (probably seven pairs) were taken, because there were to be blood sacrifices.

When Noah came out of the ark, his first act was to build an altar and kill at least one of every kind of clean animals and birds (8:20). He could not have done this, if there had been only one pair.

Verse 7: And Noah went in

It was a tremendous act of faith. The people round about must have thought that his folly had now reached its climax. We do not know what they thought when suddenly the animals began entering.

But we do know that Noah's entering the ark became the grounds for the condemnation of the world (Hebrews 11:7). No man could say that he could not believe. A believing convict condemns an unbelieving convict. A believing doctor condemns an unbelieving doctor. The entering in of the believer condemns the unbeliever.

Verse 10: It came to pass

Enoch had prophesied and had announced the judgment upon the ungodly. His son Methuselah showed the patience of God in his long life. He died just a short while before it came to pass. Noah announced it and built the vast Ark in the sight of the world, which undoubtedly ridiculed him. He held steadfast to the end in spite of all appearances and without any precedent whatsoever. At last judgment came to pass. God is not a man that He should lie. All that He has promised He will perform.

Verse 15: They went unto Noah into the ark

I once read a railing article which ridiculed the idea of Noah catching all the animals and what a time he must have had. But the Lord God can turn the heart of animals as He wishes. The earth had not yet been divided into continents and the animals were nearby. None of them had yet tasted blood, and the Lord brought them to the Ark.

Only man is more stupid than the animals: "The ox knows its owner, and the ass its master's crib; but Israel does not know, my people does not understand" (Isaiah 1:3, RSV).

Verse 16: God had commanded . . . the Lord shut him in

Once more God shows more than one side of His nature and being. As God, *Elohim,* He commanded. As Jehovah, the Redeemer, He shut Noah in. There was safety indeed. The shutting in of Noah is the equivalent of our being sealed with the Holy Spirit (Ephesians 4:30). Noah was not only saved, he was safe and secure.

Verse 17: The waters . . . bare up the ark

The same waters that destroyed life on the earth bore up the ark in which Noah and all his family were carried safely. The same judgment that swept down from God upon the Lord Jesus Christ brings death to those who refuse and life to those who believe. In the ark Noah was surrounded by judgment which showed God's hatred of sin, but he himself was safe. In Christ we are surrounded by the judgment of God against sin, and we are safe.

The Ark . . . was lift up high above the earth

If you could have looked upon this earth from the moon, you would have seen vast rolling waves destroying every living thing on the earth. But on the surface, like a cork bobbing on a stream, you would have seen the Ark with its precious cargo. It is possible to get away from the earth and to look at the world in judgment by standing in the Word of God.

Verse 22: All that was in the dry land

Never go beyond what is written. Darrow cynically confused Bryan by asking him if he believed every word in the Bible. When the great commoner replied that he did, Darrow asked contemptuously if he believed that the fish had drowned in the flood. Bryan did not know how to answer, made one of his great speeches, and died the next day. If he had known the little intricacies of the Word, he could have confounded the skeptic. Only the animals that had within them the breath of life died. Only that which was on dry land died.

Genesis 8

Verse 1: God remembered Noah

If God had not remembered Noah, He would not have been God. He would have been unfaithful to the promises made to Adam and Eve in the Garden of Eden and He would have been guilty of destroying the seed of the woman which was to bruise the serpent's head. "But God's firm foundation" — that without which we could not conceive of God — "stands, bearing this seal: 'The Lord knows those who are his'" (II Timothy 2:19, RSV). "If we are faithless, he remains faithful, for he cannot deny himself" (II Timothy 2:13, RSV). If God had not remembered Noah, all that Noah would have lost would have been his soul, but God would have lost His honor.

Verse 4: And the ark rested

Back to the judged earth came the Ark with its life and promise. God's plan was bound up in it, and its inhabitants were to continue the life that He would ordain. The word *Ararat* in Hebrew means "holy ground." Only legend links this name with any geographical location. It might have been on the top of the Mount of Olives, or in any other place of God's choice. We may be sure its timbers are not resting in ruins anywhere.

Verses 7, 8: A raven . . . a dove

We know from other parts of the Scripture that the dove is a symbol of the Holy Spirit, for in this form He came on Christ at His baptism. Perhaps, therefore, we are justified in looking upon the raven as representing the man of the flesh who goes out into the judged world, seemingly satisfied with what he finds there. The dove kept returning to the Ark for its food until it was time for all to go forth.

Verses 15, 16: Then God spake unto Noah saying, Go forth

Not until he had orders from God did Noah move. He did not follow the counsel of his intelligence, though the absence of the dove might have caused him to act prematurely. He knew that the Ark had grounded, but he did not follow his natural curiosity. He waited on God. The Lord is never before His time and He is never behind. His appointments are certain.

Verse 20: And Noah builded an altar

Once more the scarlet cord is seen in the Scripture. Blood had to be shed. The world had been judged, but Noah knew that all the evil nature of Adam had gone into the Ark and that same evil nature had come out of the Ark. Fellowship with God must be maintained by the constant reminder of the creature's sinfulness and the substitute's death for that sin. Now we see why seven of the clean beasts were taken into the Ark. Life in the new world was to be based on faith in the substitutionary atonement. Blood was to be shed. There was still but one way to God as there always would be but one way.

Verse 21: The Lord smelled a sweet savour

The altar had been built to Jehovah, and it is Jehovah who accepts the sacrifice. The faith and obedience of Noah in understanding and performing that which was the symbol of Christ's death was well-pleasing to God. In simple fashion Noah was showing the Lord's death in this pageant.

The Lord was not looking upon the actual altar and sacrifices, but upon Mount Calvary and the Lord Jesus Christ, dying there for sinners. It is Christ and only Christ who is acceptable to God, and our acceptance is in Him.

I will not again curse

Once the object lesson has been set forth, there is no need to repeat it. There could be no change in the sinful nature of man. If God had cursed the ground every time man sinned, there would have been a continuing curse, flowing like a river.

This, too, illustrates the fact that Christ, having died for sin once, dies no more. And it demonstrates that Christ having paid our debt, not even God can seek to collect it a second time from us. He died once, for all, and forever. Judgment cannot break out twice against the same transgressions. It is finished.

Verse 22: While the earth remaineth

The unchanging round of the seasons is now set in motion by God. A set of laws that is to be unvarying is established.

Genesis 9

Verse 1: And God blessed Noah and his sons

As Adam had been the head of the race in its first beginning, Noah is now the head of the race in its new beginning. This new start is marked by blessing from the first moment. God's holiness and hatred of sin had been manifested in His judgment upon the sin of the world, and all was now moving under sovereign grace. God is with them in their new beginning and His presence is blessing. The God who said, "Come into the ark" (7:1), not, "Go into the ark," and who went with them through the waters of judgment, will be with them in the new life that now begins.

Be fruitful, and multiply, and replenish the earth

Again God gives the command for fruitfulness. This does not refer, merely, to the reproduction of the species, but to fruitfulness in every good work before God (Colossians 1:10). Man is not here on earth to live according to his whim, but to live in accordance with God's plan. To be blessed by God is to be doubly responsible before Him. To obey the exhortation to be fruitful is to know the power of the blessing.

Verse 2: The fear of you

God had given to Adam dominion over all the animal creation, but man had fallen low. Now God assures Noah of his safety and his power by putting fear and dread of man into the heart of the brute creation. Sin was leaving a deeper and deeper mark, but the grace of God was rising higher and higher. If we compare this passage with 1:29, it would seem that man was a vegetarian before the Flood and that now meat enters his diet by the command of God.

Verse 4: The life thereof, which is the blood thereof

Here is the first indication in Scripture of the nature of the blood, and the foreshadowing of the atonement. Blood was shed when the first pair were given garments of skins, but now God gives the revelation which will be more fully expressed in the law, "For the life of the flesh is in the blood; and I have given it to you upon the altar to make atonement for your souls; for it is the blood that maketh an atonement for the soul" (Leviticus 17:11).

The sacredness of life taught here is not to be carried to the Satanic extreme of Hinduism, for God wants man to see death in animals and to live by feeding upon death, as a constant reminder that we live and move and have our being through His death.

Verse 5: Surely will I require

The sovereignty of God is a doctrine that should fill us with awe. God is supreme and we are His creatures. Even those who remain creatures and refuse to become sons through Christ are subject to His ordinances and laws and must give an account to Him for all things. We are subject, and will one day give an account even for the air that we breathe and how we expel it past our vocal cords in words.

Verse 6: By man shall his blood be shed

Man failed when innocent. He was unable to live by conscience after receiving the knowledge of good and evil. God now proceeds to block off another of his excuses. Man might have said, "Things have become so bad because Cain wasn't properly dealt with. If we had had a town meeting and exercised the weight of public opinion in judgment, we could have brought righteousness." "I shall now put that idea to the test," God replies, "I hereby institute the reign of human authority. I commit to man the right of the death penalty."

Here was the beginning of human government and it will not succeed in justifying man because anything that man touches is defiled.

In the image of God made He man

Only in an accommodated sense can this phrase be applied to all men, for the image was clearly defaced in the Fall, and there are only the vestigial remnants of that creation. But even the lowest man is yet a trinity — body, soul and spirit — and this puts him above the vegetable life with body, and the animal life with body and soul. But man possesses the spirit of man which is the searching light of the Lord (Proverbs 20:27). This explains the great sacredness of human life, and, also is the reason for our obligation of life as men with a triune nature.

Verse 9: I establish my covenant with you

Man has no claim whatsoever on God, any more than a cup has a claim on the potter who formed it. God gave man life and God continues to keep man in life, and man is dependent upon God for every breath he draws. But God has been pleased to bind Himself by voluntary agreements called covenants in order that man may learn that God is full of grace and may serve Him with thanksgiving.

God made a covenant with Adam to give him blessings that he did not merit in himself. Now that the world has undergone the judgment of the Flood, God makes a covenant with Noah and the creation, confirming it by a sign. He who by justice should have destroyed, was moved by love and grace to give pardon and promise instead of wrath.

Verse 10: With every living creature

The covenant with Adam included all men; that with Abraham included all who believe; that with Moses applied to the Jewish nation, but even the lowliest bird, reptile and insect had a place in the promise made to Noah. It was a creature covenant, without any spiritual blessings. It promised a surcease of physical judgment until the end of time.

As a result of this covenant, mankind has sunk back into apathy and counts itself free from restraint. Man does what he pleases and God, seemingly, takes no notice of it. The covenant, therefore, reveals the sinful heart of man who is always willing to sin against grace. To those who say that a prohibition excites man to disobedience, God demonstrates that freedom from restraint does the same thing.

63

Verse 12: This is the token

The sinful heart of man understands that judgment was well merited. Men see the fiercest outbreaks of their neighbors and know the depths of their own hearts and have moments of looking up in terror.

But when the storm beats most fiercely upon the earth, there is the rainbow to remind them that God has promised never again to destroy the earth by a flood, and that the round of seasons will continue to the end. It does not change man, for he always despises the riches of God's goodness, forbearance, and longsuffering, not knowing that this goodness was calculated to lead him to repentance (Romans 2:4).

Verse 13: I do set my bow in the cloud

This is another little detail in the evidence that there was no rain on the earth before the Flood, or the rainbow would have appeared then also. But now there has come the great climactic change and God, who is light, and in whom dwells no darkness at all, will shine through His own rainstorms and reflect to the eyes of man the prism of His own glory, for there is a rainbow around the throne of God (Revelation 4:3). At the moment that rain was falling, the sign of the rainbow would assure sinners that the forbearance of God was reigning, and that they were under the grace of God.

Verse 15: I will remember my covenant

The glory of God is shown by the things which He remembers and by those which He forgets. He remembers His covenant, but our sins and our iniquities He will remember no more (Jeremiah 31:34). The analogy is perfect. The flood of judgment has fallen upon Christ and carried Him to death while we have been placed, snug and safe, in the ark of His love. Those who do not believe in the eternal security of the believer tear the rainbow from the covenant of God, and make Him a liar (I John 5:10).

Verse 16: I will look upon it

God never repeats Himself merely for effect. In verse 15 God said He would remember His covenant. Now He says that He will look upon the rainbow in order to remember His covenant.

That is to tell us that grace is in the sight of God, and that we are sure. God does not look upon us in ourselves; He looks upon Christ and we are accepted in the Beloved.

Verse 18: The sons of Noah

The evil that was in the earth and which had drawn forth the anger of God against the race was also within the Ark in the hearts of Noah and his sons and in the hearts of the four wives. Even the grace of God does not change the roots of sin that are within man; instead it plants the new roots of grace. Even God does not deal with the old, unregenerate heart: He declares it to be incurable (Jeremiah 17:9, Heb.), and gives us a new heart.

Verse 21: And he . . . was drunken

I can never read this verse without remembering that the Holy Spirit, in the New Testament, has recorded Noah as "a preacher of righteousness" (II Peter 2:5). It is a great illustration of the fact that many men in the Bible who were strong for God when they were young departed far from the will of God when they were older. It is a proof that past work does not furnish power for future victory.

And he was uncovered

According to some theology, Noah would have been lost at this moment. But according to the eternal covenants of God's grace, Noah was covered by the righteousness of God even when the nature of his sinful nature was most clearly visible in all its folly. He could have said with David, "I was stupid and ignorant, I was like a beast toward thee" (Psalm 73:22, RSV).

In the New Testament records there is no breath of any of this scandal: God who remembers His covenants also forgets man's sins. Noah is listed among the heroes of faith, and is given the glorious title of "preacher of righteousness," and counted as "heir of righteousness" (Hebrews 11:7).

Verses 22, 25: Ham . . . cursed be Canaan

Just as Jonah was given a great task to do after his flight and his folly, so Noah is given a new opportunity to be the mouthpiece of God. The circumstances of his sin are made the framework of the prophecy which God speaks through him. The man who was drunk with wine is now filled with the Spirit (Ephesians

5:18). He is now covered with the garment of prophecy and speaks forth the will and the Word of God.

It is necessary to right a great wrong at this point. Never in all history, until the middle of the nineteenth century, did anyone imagine that Ham was the father of the Negro peoples and that there was a curse upon him. Prejudiced souls who wished to justify their investments in human flesh resorted to any subterfuge to bolster their untenable position. The Hamites were the Egyptians, Babylonians, Hittites, Canaanites, Phoenicians, Carthagenians; but not the Negroes. Moreover, the curse was pronounced on Ham through one of his sons — Canaan. Any attempt to make black skin the fulfillment of this curse is unscholarly, prejudiced to the extreme and certainly without basis in the Bible.

Verse 26: Blessed be the Lord God of Shem

The blessing is not upon Shem, but upon the God of Shem. Nothing can take root in man. It is the God of Shem who will bring forth Christ from Shem.

Genesis 10

Verse 1: These are the generations

Some may wonder what is the value of long lists of unpronounceable names in the Old Testament. When I visited the great machine shops of the Panama Canal Zone, perhaps the most complete in the world, I was told of tools there that had never been used and that they hoped never would be used. If a lock were bombed, there would be urgent need of repairs and there could be no waiting for spare parts from the States. There were tools used every day and some never used.

There may be verses in the Scriptures that are used, spiritually, every day, but chapters like this one have frequently confounded the critics and proved the accuracy of the Word.

Verse 8: Nimrod . . . he began to be a mighty one in the earth

Hidden under the poor English translation is a horrible story of desperate rebellion against God. God had pronounced a curse upon Ham, and now Satan raises Nimrod, king of Babylon and descendant of Ham, to nullify the curse of God. The Hebrew reads, "And Cush begat Nimrod, he began to be a mighty tyrant in the land. He was a terrible subjugator, defiant before the face of Jehovah; wherefore it is said: Even as Nimrod, the giant hunter, presumptuous in the presence of Jehovah . . . ."

Here is the beginning of human dictatorship and organized rebellion against God. Collective man will prove no better than individual man.

Verse 10: The beginning of His kingdom was Babel

But the end of human rebellion is Babylon the great, the

67

mother of harlots. And as we study the book of Revelation we see religious Babylon, political Babylon and commercial Babylon all coming under the judgment of God.

Man may think that his affairs are succeeding because they have the first flush of success. But God does not settle His accounts when men reap the first harvest. "Though the mills of God grind slowly, yet they grind exceeding small."

The whole purpose of history is to demonstrate that there is no possible solution to any problems through man, but that only God's wisdom and power can bring righteousness.

Verse 11: And Calah

This, one of the cities of rebellion, was so completely destroyed that its memory was lost to the ages and critics even denied its existence. Then in 1845, Sir Austen Henry Layard discovered the ruins of the city, and from this began the development of our knowledge of the archaeology of this part of the world. But it wasn't the discovery of Calah that proved the Bible; the Bible all along had been the proof of Calah's existence, even more than its rocks and stones — for these shall pass away but the Word shall not pass away (Matthew 24:35).

Verse 25: In his days was the earth divided

Nimrod was the first to attempt a "united nations" against God. It was the first of many attempts, all of which are doomed to failure and judgment. God brought judgment upon the united nations and divided the earth so that nationalities, peoples and languages came into being on the earth.

Some have thought that this verse is the clue to what is known as "continental drift," that the land masses of the earth, originally together, began to separate at this time, and people with original ideas of truth went into every quarter of the globe. Thus we have the origin of all the pagan myths that parallel the truth of God.

Verse 32: By these were the nations divided

One of the foremost Orientalists in modern times has said that this is the most important chapter in the Bible for the student of ancient history. Its accuracy is recognized by friend and foe alike. The earliest movements of history are recorded here. Gomer has given us the Germanic peoples, Madai speaks of the

Medes, Javan is another spelling for Ionia — Greece. It is impossible to understand the movements of the peoples in the rest of Genesis without referring to this chapter. This is authentic history, in fact, it is the beginning of human history.

Genesis 11

Verse 1: One language, and of one speech

God has tested man under every conceivable condition and found him wanting. In our day there are those who think that bettering man's environment will help him; they forget the environment of Eden. Others think that education will save man, forgetting that knowledge was received in the Fall and that conscience failed to keep man righteous. Still others think that something like the United Nations can enforce righteousness in the world.

But here in Babylon those conditions existed, and were a spur to blasphemous rebellion, and not to righteousness. The Bible does not teach, merely, that man fell once in Eden, but that man always falls when confronted with fresh conditions that are calculated to reveal what he truly is.

Verses 3, 4: Let us . . . let us . . . let us . . .

The clue to every action is whether it proceeds from the will of man or from the will of God. Man in rebellion says, "Let us"; man in submission says, "Thy will be done."

Put your hands out in front of you, palms down as though to grasp something. That is the attitude of taking. Now turn your hands over, palms up. That is the attitude of receiving.

Perhaps the whole key to life's story lies in the fact in saying, "Let *me*," instead of "Lord, do it all." The terrible thing about the former prayer is that God lets man do what he wants to do, and then there comes failure and frustration. God's ways are ways of pleasantness, and all His paths are peace (Proverbs 3:17).

Verse 4: A tower whose top may reach unto heaven

The translators have obscured the sense by giving us an idea that men were attempting to build a tower that would reach all the way to heaven. They would have been doubly fools to start it by the river when there were mountains in sight a few miles away that would have given them a great start.

The fact is: The tower was a ziggurat on top of which was a zodiac by which the priests hoped to get knowledge from the stars. It was an open, defiant turning to Satan and the beginning of devil worship. This is why the Bible everywhere pronounces a curse on those who consult the sun, the moon, and the stars of heaven.

Verse 5: The Lord came down to see the city

There are many indications in the Scriptures that the Lord is not only aware of all that goes on upon this earth, whether of good or ill, but that He is vitally interested in all that takes place.

He was interested in the daydreams of David, the shepherd boy (Psalm 132:2-6). Not a sparrow falls without His knowledge, and the very hairs of our heads are numbered (Matthew 10: 29, 30). "His eyes behold, his eyelids test, the children of men" (Psalm 11:4). Shall He not then come down to see the first city of rebellion?

Verse 6: Nothing will be restrained from them

When men begin by running after Satan, they will end by wishing to dethrone God. They had started a city because they did not want to obey the command of God to replenish the earth, which would have meant separation from each other, and going to widely remote places.

Thus they imagined that by binding themselves together they would be able to organize strong enough to procure their own will. The imagination which was only evil continually before the Flood is still with the race, and they are imagining to replace God. "Let us break His bands asunder," is the cry.

Verse 7: Let us . . . confound their language

The Lord stopped work on the city and the tower in the most

unlooked-for manner. They might have anticipated difficulties through quarrels among themselves or by judgments from heaven in fire or flood, but a miracle in their brains and vocal cords had never occurred to them. Thus God confounds the worldly imaginations of men. Henceforward every time they opened their mouths to speak, there was the reminder of their disunity and failure.

The multiple earphones in the meetings of the "united" nations are a testimony of the impiety of the fathers of the nations. Tongues that were divided at Babel were given as a witness at Pentecost and will one day be united in blessing at His return.

Verse 8: They left off to build the city

Those who go their own way will always end in frustration. There is no real peace except in the way of the Lord's direction and leading. How many men could testify that the thing they grasped at became a bubble in their hands, and the fruit they sought turned to ashes in their mouths. God has many ways to make bitter the things for which men give their lives and He must always do it when something is prized beyond Himself.

Verse 9: From thence did the Lord scatter them

God always has His way in the end. It is impossible that the eternal counsels of the Godhead should not be fulfilled. If a man wants to kick against the pricks, he may have success for a while and make a name for himself in the earth, but in the end he is brought either to judgment or to the Damascus road. It is either man's way, ending in disappointment and failure, or it is God's way, not only ending in joy and triumph but filled with joy and triumph.

God is sovereign, and His way shall be accomplished. Here, as always, there was mercy blended with judgment. It was judgment that scattered them through the earth, but it was mercy that accompanied them with full supplies of grace.

Verse 30: But Sarai was barren; she had no child

Here is the seed from which the next eleven chapters grow. God meant all this for good, and all the testings and the triumphs of the faith of Abraham and Sarah grew out of this. God's plan and His purpose in the story of Hagar and Ishmael, the promise of Isaac, the command to offer him up, the divine deliverance, the work of providence in this family, the ultimate arrival of complete faith and the proving of God's promise, are all bound up with the fact that Sarah had no child.

Verse 31: Terah took Abram his son

Behind Terah's action was the faith of his son, Abram. God appeared to Abram and gave him the orders. It was evidently Abram's determination to go that moved Terah, his father, to join the procession. Abram was obeying God, but he acknowledged his earthly father's rightful position. It turned out to be a compromise, and Abram lost several years by allowing his father a part in the action that derived from the call and command of God. Terah was a devil worshiper, and he managed the party of which his son was a member according to his own earthly ideas and not according to the simplicity of God's command.

They came unto Haran, and dwelt there

The world has many a halfway house on the road to God's will. The order was: Destination Canaan. The execution was: long stop in Haran. Terah probably created a great emotional scene at the old home in Ur, when his son announced that God had called him to go to a far country which he had never seen. Finally, the old man said he would go too. Since he had the authority of the father, Abram deferred to his wishes and there was the long sojourn at Haran. Terah probably was very proud of his religious progress. Had he not given up Ur? Was he not well out into the desert? Could he not glory in his progress? But Terah died in Haran.

Genesis 12

Verse 1: The Lord had said unto Abram

God did not choose Abram because of anything good in Abram, but because of the love in the heart of God. And the Lord distinctly declares: "For when he was but one I called him" (Isaiah 51:2, RSV). There were others just as needy, some perhaps morally better, but God is sovereign in all that He does. The only explanation is: "Yea, Father, for such was thy gracious will" (Matthew 11:26, RSV). If God were obliged to save any man, salvation could not be by grace.

Get thee out of thy country

The reason for this is the failure of mankind on a national basis at the tower of Babel. God purposes to rule this earth in righteousness and by means of men. When the race failed as a group, God created nationality as a curse. By sovereign grace, God set up one man as the head of a nation through whom righteousness should come to the earth in the Saviour, and to whom government should one day be committed.

And from thy kindred

It seems heartless to ask a son to leave his father and family, but God was asking the son to leave a godless father and a godless family. Joshua says, "Thus says the Lord, the God of Israel, 'Your fathers lived of old beyond the Euphrates, Terah, the father of Abraham . . . and they served other gods . . . Now therefore . . . put away the gods which your fathers served . . .'" (Joshua 24:2, 14, RSV).

74

We remember that later in the days of Jacob, Rachel stole her father's idols and hid them when he searched her tent. The path of holiness is a path of separation.

From thy father's house

The hardest place to leave is home. Here is where there is security in life and the shelter of protection. If home is going to hinder dependence upon the Lord, it is best to leave it, but not in willfulness. I saw a cartoon showing a young wife saying to her young husband, "I'd leave and go home to my parents if they weren't so unreasonable also." The fact, of course, was that she was willful and wanted to go where she could have her own way.

A land that I will shew thee

It makes no difference where it is or what is its geology or geography. If the Lord leads us there, it is the land for us. If the Lord does not lead us, it can never be the right land, even though it is paved with diamonds.

Literally, Abram was being led out of the land of Ur into the land of Canaan. Spiritually, Abram was being led out into the heavenly country. He thus confessed that he was a stranger and a pilgrim in the earth. "For people who speak thus make it clear that they are seeking a homeland. If they had been thinking of that land from which they had gone out, they would have had opportunity to return. But as it is, they desire a better country, that is, a heavenly one. Therefore God is not ashamed to be called their God" (Hebrews 11:14-16, RSV).

Verse 2: I will make of thee a great nation

This is the first of the unconditional promises. If God's promises had conditions, they would never have been fulfilled, for we do not have the power to keep any condition. Therefore, the promises must be in pure grace, and without conditions. "I will make of thee a great nation." "But Lord," Abraham might have said, "suppose I get out of Thy will, or my posterity should become idolators, or my descendants should crucify Thy Son?" "I will make of thee a great nation." The promise is not because of what Abraham might or might not do or be, but because of God's grace and His design.

I will bless thee

But Lord, suppose Abraham becomes a liar; and his grand-son, Jacob, becomes a crook; also his greatest son, David, be-comes an adulterer and a murderer; and the nation descended from Abraham becomes so evil that it is necessary to scatter them in judgment throughout the earth? "I will bless you." But can man's sin never make Thee a liar? "I will bless you." Why, Lord? "Because I am the God of whom it is said: 'If we are faithless, he remains faithful — for he cannot deny himself'" (II Timothy 2:13). This is unmerited grace.

And make thy name great

By the thousands, Jews, Mohammedans and Christians have been named Abraham. Abraham is one of the few universal names. But the greatness involved in the promise was not merely that the literal name would be widely used. Abram was to become Abraham and thus be the father of many nations, both a physical seed in the nation and a spiritual seed in the church.

The act of leaving Ur and going to the land of Canaan would give him the other name — Hebrew — which means "one who crossed over." And, most of all, Abraham is the name that is bound up with all the promises of God. The name is found seventy-four times in the New Testament.

Thou shalt be a blessing

The only possible way in which a man who is of the lost race of Adam can be a blessing to another is that he will become a channel by which God will pour Himself out through the man. Human breath is foul and can carry only the miasma of death. But the Holy Spirit — the Holy Breath — can come through the throat of a man and bring blessing to multitudes because it is the breath of God, pure and undefiled. God used Abraham as a nest in which to hatch out all the divine principles of salva-tion by grace and thus he became a blessing.

Verse 3: I will bless them that bless thee

Only eternity will reveal how true this has been in the history of the nations. Only the Gibeonites were spared when Israel entered the land of Canaan, for they sought to make a covenant with God's people. I believe that the Lord has blessed the

United States because this nation is a haven for the persecuted Jews.

In the future, at the judgment of the nations, it is written that the Lord Jesus Christ will say to the nations on His right hand, "As you did it to one of the least of these my brethren, you did it to me" (Matthew 25:40). His brethren, of course, are the children of Abraham living at that day; and the passage takes on its real meaning when seen in this light.

Curse him that curseth thee

When a man dies, a physician has to write on the death certificate the cause of death. When a nation dies, more often than not, the cause of death is that the nation has mistreated the Jews. When Ham rebelled against Shem, one by one, the tribes of Ham were destroyed or reduced to a minor state: Egypt, Canaan, the Hittites. When the Greeks overran Palestine and desecrated the altar in the Jewish temple, they were soon conquered by Rome. When Rome killed Paul and many others, and destroyed Jerusalem under Titus, Rome soon fell. Spain was reduced to a fifth-rate nation after the Inquisition against the Jews; Poland fell after the pogroms; Hitler's Germany went down after its orgies of anti-Semitism; Britain lost her empire when she broke her faith with Israel.

In thee shall all families of the earth be blessed

Here is another great promise of the Saviour. For, even as unborn Levi was in the loins of Abraham (Hebrews 7:10), so the humanity of the Lord Jesus was in the loins of Abraham.

Thus some will be saved in every people — and we stress the literalness of the word — in every tribe, in every tongue, in every people and in every nation (Revelation 5:9). No tribe is so remote that it will not be reached and touched by the God of Abraham, who will pluck brands from the burning out of every family of men.

Verse 4: So Abram departed, as the Lord had spoken unto him

It is a great thing to obey God, and to obey Him meticulously. The fact that Abram allowed his old father to go along with him at first, perhaps allowing the neighbors to think that Terah was managing the expedition (11:31), is now passed over. Only the obedience of faith is in view here. When the Lord tells the story in the eleventh chapter of Hebrews, there is no hint of the delayed obedience, it is one straight account of Abraham's travels, and it reads, "By faith Abraham obeyed when he was called to go out" (Hebrews 11:8).

Lot went with him

Of all the idolators of the land of Ur, it would seem that only Lot caught the same vision given to Abraham and Sarah. Lot believed God. Something in the faith and life of his uncle Abraham showed him the glory that had been revealed to Abraham, and Lot would go with Abraham to the end.

Lot would not be as strong as Abraham; he would cause Abraham a lot of trouble; he would not even be able to save his wife and children, but he himself would be justified, and reach the heavenly land as well as the land of Canaan.

Verse 5: They went forth . . . they came

There was no dallying now. They started, and they arrived. The life of faith consists in pressing on to the end of the road and the goal of salvation. God had given the promise, "I will . . . I will . . . ." and these promises were unconditional. When Abram stepped out and traveled, it was the proof that he believed the "I will" of the promise.

The Holy Spirit, in the New Testament, states that the Gospel was preached to Abraham when God said, "In thee shall all nations be blessed" (Galatians 3:8).

Verse 6: The Canaanite was then in the land

These were the sons of Ham, and they intended to oppose the way of God's people at every step. There is more here than meets the eye, for the word "afterward" of Genesis 6:4 tells of demons and their attempt to possess man for the cause of Satan. They were in Canaan to block the way of promise.

Verse 7: And the Lord appeared unto Abram

There were to be great trials, great struggles and great blessings. The Lord who called Abraham at the beginning now appears to him as he enters the land. It is always so. New supplies of grace will meet us at every point in the conflict.

A nation may put soldiers on the field of battle without sufficient ammunition and supplies; but with God there is always more than enough, and there is Himself. God has never required anything of a believer that he has not already furnished. God demands righteousness and provides Christ. God demands conflict and comes Himself to fight for the believer (Exodus 14:14).

Unto thy seed

The New Testament tells us that God was not promising something solely to the physical descendants of Abraham, but that He was promising it to Christ. "Now the promises were made to Abraham and to his offspring. It does not say, 'And to offsprings,' referring to many; but, referring to one, 'And to your offspring,' which is Christ" (Galatians 3:16, RSV).

In modern language it would be: God, party of the first part, makes a promise to Abraham and Christ, joint parties of the second part . . . But suppose that Abraham goes bankrupt? That makes no difference as long as Christ remains solvent. The promises are sure because they were made between God the Father and God the Son.

The New Testament quotes this passage in order to remark that God knew the difference between one and more than one, and that He used the singular here and not the plural because He was talking about Christ, and not about Israel.

This is great teaching on the nature of the Bible. Some insist that the thoughts and not the words are inspired. Satan hates the doctrine of verbal inspiration because he knows that such a belief is the true point on the sword of the Spirit, which is the Word of God. If he can break off the point of the Word of God, he will save himself many a cut. Everyone who denies the verbal inspiration plays into the devil's hands. God says that He knows how to count and that He has sense enough to set down exactly what He means.

There built he an altar

In the place of the appearance of the presence of God, stood the altar which signified sacrifice, worship and communion. Back in Ur God had told Abram to go "to a land that I will show you." Now Abram has seen it and God says, "this land I will *give* to your descendants." Abram builds an altar, for there is worship and communion that goes with the gifts and promises of God.

Here is the first time in the Bible that God is said to have appeared to anyone. He *called* and *spoke* to Adam, Cain, Noah and Abram, but now to faith which has obeyed comes a manifestation of the presence of God that calls forth special worship.

Verse 8: He removed from thence

Abram by now was learning that the life of faith is a life of pilgrimage. From Ur to Haran, from Haran to Sichem and Moreh. Then to Bethel, from plain to mountain. God may call some of His children to settle down temporarily, but others He calls to a life of pilgrimage. Even though we have a house and ground, remember that we are pilgrims. The only land Abram ever bought was a burying place. He looked for a city which has foundations, whose builder and maker is God (Hebrews 11:10).

The true believer will never have his heaven in a bank; he will always have his bank in heaven. Stocks, bonds, and deeds may be possessed, but they will never possess the yielded believer.

And pitched his tent . . . he builded an altar

A tent and an altar. This was all that Abram ever had. To the end of his life he was what men call a nomad, but he was walking with God and teaching us that the life of faith is subject to change without notice. Back in the land of the Chaldees, his brother Nahor built a city and called it after his own name (Genesis 24:10). The world might have considered Nahor a success and Abram a failure, but with God it was the other way around.

Our old nature which we inherited from Adam may delight in outward things and settle down in and of the world, but the spirit that is given us by God will have no certain dwelling place, but our abiding will be in Him. As long as we have the altar with our tent, we have all that is necessary.

Verse 9: And Abram journeyed

In the next verse we shall see that his ultimate destination was Egypt; but what was his point of departure? He left Bethel, which means "the house of God," and in so traveling he left his altar, his place of worship. Here was the root cause of all the evils that followed. If he soon landed in Egypt, in the midst of

80

lying, compromise, disobedience and dishonor, it was because he had left the altar and the place of his worship.

The Ephesian church strayed out of the will of God by leaving its first love (Revelation 2:4). Any believer who is in the Egypt of bondage today can know that he is there because he has left his Bethel.

Verse 10: There was a famine in the land

God had brought Abram all the way from Ur, not in order to let him die of hunger. The famine was to test and strengthen the faith by which Abram was learning to walk. Faith is not a mushroom that grows overnight in damp soil; it is an oak tree that grows for a thousand years under the blast of the wind and rain.

But it must be made manifest that even the faith of Abram is nothing without the God of Abram. Faith is not a work to be regarded but a gift to be developed. After all of the unconditional promises, there was the promise of daily blessing, conditional upon dwelling in the land. Abram fails in this test by not trusting God to keep His honor pure in taking care of the pilgrim whom He has brought so far.

Abram went down into Egypt

Like a coin that has a head and a tail, every event in life has a side that can draw us to God and a side that can draw us away from God. The famine was just such an event. If Abram had seen it as a bulwark for his faith, he would have stayed in the land on full rations until the last mouthful was eaten, and then he could have expected God to rain food from heaven. God would have had to do this to keep His promise.

In olden days both sides of the events were called temptations, but now only the downward side is so called. This explains the contradiction between the statement that God tempts no man (James 1:13), that is, draws no man downward, and the prayer, "Lead us not into temptation" (Matthew 6:13). This latter verse means: Lord, do not expose us to tests that have two sides, for we will always go down if left to ourselves. Do not put us to the test. When God does not answer that prayer, but permits us to be tested, it is never more than we are able to meet (I Corinthians 10:13).

81

The famine was grievous

The Canaanite held the land, and then the famine stripped it. Still it was the land of promise. It is so with every phase of our lives. The enemy will always oppose us, and the famine will teach us that the land is a land of promise; and not a land of present contentment. At times the walk with God will be such that even faith will hardly know where to turn.

We may think it strange that such a fiery trial should be needed, or that the promised rest should yet be kept from us by others, and the Lord's enemies. Yet such is the path; for the question is — Can we be satisfied with God? And many a weary step is trodden before we have made this attainment.

Egypt

Abram had come a thousand miles by faith and he now walks into failure. Whenever there is victory by faith, there is always a new and more difficult trial. It takes more grace to stay in Canaan than it does to get there. Peter had faith to step out of the boat onto the waters, but he did not have faith to walk to Jesus.

Every act of faith brings us into greater trials where more faith and grace are needed. The grace is there (I Corinthians 10:13) but it takes time to become acquainted with it. The way of God is really a series of terraces, each higher than the one before, and each presenting new dangers, new supplies, and new knowledge.

Verse 13: Say . . . thou art my sister

One failure leads to another. If we depart from the will of God at even a small angle, the distance between our road and the Lord's will increase. Abram, who had walked by faith all the way from Ur to Canaan, began to walk by the circumstances of famine. Then, without asking counsel of the Lord, he took a second step to avoid further trial. Having forgotten the counsel and care of the Lord, he forgot the promise of God concerning the seed which was to come. Abram allowed his wife to go into the palace of Ham, where, if it had not been for the intervention of God, her womb might have been contaminated by a Satan-dominated king.

82

Verse 17: The Lord plagued Pharaoh

This was divine intervention at an opportune moment. Sarah was to be the mother of the faithful. She was the freewoman, a type of salvation by grace (Galatians 4:22-24). Abram should have been her protector, for he was her lord (I Peter 3:6), but having turned from the care and counsel of God, he allowed himself to be wooed by temporal advantages, receiving flocks, herds and servants.

But when God intervened and plagued the house of Pharaoh, Abram suffered the shame and humiliation of a man, who having been an ambassador for God, was sent away like a dog with his tail between his legs. It was not a pretty sight, but the effects of sin are never pretty.

Genesis 13

Verse 1: So Abram went up out of Egypt

Our God is the God of the second opportunity — and of the seventy-second. We can always begin afresh with the God of grace. We are the people of God and Abraham is the father of all who believe. God's dealings with him are a pattern of what we may expect from our Father.

We often go down into Egypt and God always waits for us to return. He creates difficulties for us in Egypt so that we may long for the grapes of His land and the blessings of His communion. Swine-husks are often the *hors d'oeuvres* before the fatted calf. The only way to get back into the will of God is to go back to the very cause of the departure, confess it, forsake it, and return to the place of fellowship.

Verse 2: And Abram was very rich

The devil might have complained to God that Abram was faithful only because he was blessed, but now there begins the story of the man who had riches and despised them. Abram's eyes were on the stars and the promises while the things of earth would be worth less and less to him.

As time went on, there would be many instances of his disdain of earthly possessions. This will ever be the mark of the man who has seen the Lord and is following in the paths of righteousness. The rich man is not told to abandon his wealth, but he is not to be haughty or to trust in uncertain riches (I Timothy 6:17). When the salary goes up, the love of money should go down.

84

Verse 3: And . . . went on his journey . . . even to Bethel

We remember the familiar words, "He restores my soul. He leads me in paths of righteousness for his name's sake" (Psalm 23:3, RSV). All Christians get out of the will of God at times, and many remain out for long periods. That is why God has given us such minute details of His process of restoration. Bethel is always where we left it.

Jacob had to return from Padan-aram, Moses wandered for forty years in Midian, David defiled himself with lust and blood, Jonah ran from the service of God, Peter denied the Lord with oaths and cursings, Thomas was loud in his doubting, Paul shaved his head and was ready to have a Jewish sacrifice offered for sins.

Verse 4: Place of altar, which he had made there at the first

Abram had to retrace his steps. He had to go back to the place where his tent had been at the beginning. The picture of the grace of God is wonderful, but the thought of the time lost is fearful. The return journey is always obligatory.

To the church that had left its first love God said, "Remember then from what you have fallen [the place of communion], repent and do the works you did at first" (Revelation 2:5, RSV). Every day away from the altar of communion is a wasted day.

The Word of God concerning the Nazarite is unspeakably solemn, "He shall consecrate unto the Lord the days of his separation, and shall bring a lamb . . . but the days that were before shall be lost, because his separation was defiled" (Numbers 6:12).

Abram called on the name of the Lord

It is certain that Abram had little knowledge of the meaning of the name Jehovah, for God flatly states that Abraham did not know Him by that name (Exodus 6:3).

There is a great deal of difference between a capital letter and a small letter. God had promised a Deliverer and man had been looking for a deliverer. Men knew that a jehovah was coming, but they did not know that it was to be Jehovah, God Himself. But Abraham, who knew God by His name of God Almighty, was presenting the idea of grace and redemption to God in his prayers, and was trusting in God alone.

God does not reward us according to our intelligence but

85

according to His grace. Any smallest groping in His direction finds Him.

Verse 5: And Lot also . . . had flocks

Abram had flocks but the flocks did not have him; Lot had flocks and the flocks possessed him. It is a terrible thing when a Christian is possessed by his possessions. The love of money is the root of all evil (I Timothy 6:10).

Lot is in heaven, because he was justified (II Peter 2:7), but he is the father of all the mean-minded, close-fisted, money-loving men who put things before God. His story, as it unfolds, is one of sadness and loss. He was saved, yet so as by fire, with all his works burned away (I Corinthians 3:15). Since it is possible to be in heaven without a crown (I Corinthians 9:27; Revelation 3:11), God exhorts us to take heed, and to beware.

Verse 6: The land was not able to bear them

Abram now obeys a great principle of New Testament love. "Let each of you look not only to his own interests, but also to the interests of others" (Philippians 2:4, RSV). It is the unselfish thing to do, but it shows that the life of Christ is within us when we do this.

In this action, Abram resembled the Lord Jesus Christ who "came not to be served but to serve, and to give his life as a ransom for many" (Matthew 20:28, RSV). When this scene was completed, Abram was immediately visited by God, given renewed promises and sent in to the actual possession of all that he saw. So it is that every true believer, who will deny himself for the sake of the Lord, will receive present consolation and eternal joy.

Dwell together

Only so many sheep can graze to an acre, so something must give when there are two flocks in close proximity. There is, of course, land enough and pasture enough if Abram and Lot separate, and this separation, which should have taken place in Ur of the Chaldees (Genesis 12:1) now occurs.

God is teaching us to be like Abram, and to put Him even before ties of blood. We should learn to regard all circumstances as coming from the ministering heart of God, for herein lies much of the meaning of the ordinary round of life. God uses details to test us, to reveal our weaknesses, and to lead us to places of strength.

Verse 7: There was a strife between the herdmen

Lot's meanness was communicated to his servants. They knew what would please him. The land belonged to Abram by divine gift; Lot was there by sufferance, and against the directive will of God. If Abram will let him, he will be a drag on the old saint.

Since these are the first verses in the Bible to mention wealth, they are very important. If riches are honestly obtained, held as belonging to God and used by us as stewards, they are right. But if they are falsely gained, held and used for self, they are wrong. Lot's riches are the occasion of strife. Since he is a believer, he will have to learn by losing them all. A faithful God will see that they are taken away from him.

The Canaanite and the Perizzite

It is sad when the heathen observe and know the difficulties between Christians. Abram and Lot had come into the land by the leading of the true God, and a promise had been given of blessing for all the families of the earth, but now the strife between these two believers shows the natives that these men are not unlike themselves. Many people will never listen to what any believer says because of what some believers are.

Verse 8: Let there be no strife

Servants lead little lives and fight over little things. But such strife can spread as when water is let out of a dam: the breach is small to begin with but can release a flood. Therefore, God says, "The beginning of strife is like letting out water; so quit before the quarrel breaks out" (Proverbs 17:14, RSV).

Abram has recovered from the faithlessness that drove him to Egypt when there was famine, and is ready to retire to the hills, if necessary, in order to have peace. It takes two to make a quarrel. The one who is willing to give in, *even when in the right as Abram was*, is the one who wins.

We be brethren

Abram as the leader, the elder, the one to whom God had given the promises, might have asserted his "rights," but he abandoned them. He had learned the great lesson that the only "right" we have is the right to go to hell. Everything else is ours by grace.

One who has understood this will never try to maintain his honor and his rights. He is ready to take the place of an inferior, rightly judging that condescension is the truest honor, and that to be the servant of all is to be most like our Lord. The mark of a true believer is love for the brethren (I John 3:14). Our "rights" are always safe with God.

Verse 9: Is not the whole land before thee?

From the beginning Abram has walked with God. But of Lot this is never written; it is emphasized, even, that Lot walked with Abram (12:4; 13:1, 5, etc). It is now time for Abram and Lot to separate. Abram represents the spiritual man. In his choice, Lot is representative of the natural man. If faith is to advance there must be a separation between these two. Faith must leave the choice to the natural, which always looks at things and never at God. The ground of this separation is not Egypt, for true separation does not take place while we are in the world, but after we are back at the altar, determined to go with God.

Separate thyself from me

The man who lives for the world cannot tolerate the presence of him who is determined to live for God. Even the believer who refuses to go on with God is uncomfortable in the presence of the man who dwells close to God. It is the spiritual man who recognizes the need for separation even from those who are near by ties of affection.

If thou wilt take the left hand, then I will go to the right

The servant of the Lord must not be quarrelsome (II Timothy 2:24). The true child of God can always afford to be magnanimous, simply because he is the child of God. Abram had walked with the Lord long enough to know that he would not be alone. When the Lord promises to bless us, He Himself is our blessing, and since He is with us, it makes no difference whether we go to the left or to the right.

Let the world take what seems best to it; little is much when God is in it, and walking with Him will always be all satisfaction. The providences of God are made known to us by choices that are made by others, for frequently we are given what the world considers to be the leftovers. God will be there.

Verse 10: Lot lifted up his eyes

Lot's eyes were the binoculars of his heart. The greed that was there sucked in the view of the well-watered plain, and he made the fatal choice.

It is the circumstance that reveals what a man really is. Circumstances do not make or mar a man any more than a storm fells a tree. The rot in the heart of the tree or the shallow root system is revealed by the storm, but the flaw had been there all the time waiting for the first wind to discover it to the eyes of the world.

The choices are made in the secret citadel of the heart long before the herdsmen commence to drive the cattle to the well-watered plain where all may see the shamelessness of open disgrace.

Well watered . . . before the Lord destroyed

The things which are seen are temporal (II Corinthians 4:18). The man who sees only the earthly springs has not realized how quickly the water level can fall and how quickly the judgment of God can turn all into an arid waste. The man who learns that all his springs are in the Lord (Psalm 87:7) need never fear the desert. He carries with him his own irrigation system.

The Lord Jesus said, "He who believes in me . . . Out of his heart shall flow rivers of living water" (John 7:38, RSV). Unhappy the man who looks at the surface of things. The judgment of God must fall on everything that does not have its source in Himself.

Like the land of Egypt

The mind of Lot may indeed be an illustration of nature at its best, but it should be noted that the mind not surrendered to God is always hankering after the things that faith has already given up. Abram had left Egypt behind, and forever. Lot was still comparing portions of the promised land with what he saw in Egypt and was choosing that which was most like the best in the world. Sodom was to draw the fire of God upon it because of the foulness of its inhabitants, but Lot was still judging like a babe.

Paul complained of such as Lot when he wrote the Corinthians, "But I, brethren, could not address you as spiritual men, but as men of the flesh, as babes in Christ. . . . are you not of the flesh, and behaving like ordinary men?" (I Corinthians 3:1, 3, RSV).

Verse 11: Lot chose him all the plain of Jordan

The humility, the kindness and generosity of Abiam had not melted Lot. His heart was a heart of stone. His conscience was seared as with a hot iron (I Timothy 4:2). His hard eyes had looked upon the lush country, and his greedy heart would not be moved from the choice. Lot knew well the character of the city that lay in the plain below, but the grass was green to the bellies of the cattle, and Lot found that heavenly. Like his beasts, he was ready to lie down in the wealth of the Sodom country, and like them his earthly soul was being fattened for slaughter. Abram became the father of all the faithful; Lot became the father of all the compromisers.

They separated themselves

We do not know whether Lot was a saved man at this time; certainly he was twenty years later, but he is not behaving like it now. From looking no further than this present life, we can see what an advantage love and self-denial have over selfishness. Even if Lot was gloating with glee as he contemplated his rich portion, and adding up all the riches which he hoped to have in a year or two of increase in the fertile plain, his joy could not have been as great as that of Abram, glad that he had prevented strife, that he had truly loved his nephew, that he had exhibited generosity and kindness, and that he was going to dwell in peace with God.

Verse 12: Lot . . . pitched his tent toward Sodom

One step out of the will of the Lord always leads to another. The departure from God may be by imperceptible degrees, but its end is a world away from the center of His will. Lot had begun with too great a concern about his temporal interests, and now there is too little regard for the interests of his soul.

The character of the Sodomites was well known, for they

were those described in Romans, "Though they know God's decree that those who do such things deserve to die, they not only do them but approve those who practice them" (Romans 1:32, RSV).

Verse 13: Sinners before the Lord

The most terrible characteristic of sin is that it is sin before the Lord. A sinful act may hurt the sinner and may hurt many others, but it hurts most the Lord and His desires for the good of the sinner.

David destroyed the virtue of Bathsheba, the life of Uriah, the lives of the soldiers defeated in battle, the honor of the country and the dignity of his throne; but when he repented, he cried, "Against thee, thee only, have I sinned, and done that which is evil in thy sight" (Psalm 51:4). This will be a strong deterrent from sin. The unregenerate may think that God does not see them (Psalm 10:11), but all things are naked to His sight (Hebrews 4:13).

Verse 14: The Lord said unto Abram, after that Lot was separated from him

There are some things that the Lord will never say to the unsaved. There are some things that He will not say to a baby Christian. But as the Christian advances in the life that is Christ, the Lord will speak more and more to him. Abram was the friend of God (James 2:23), and the Lord talked to him freely.

Within our hearts we have the struggle of Abram and Lot, the spiritual and the natural, and it is only when the carnal is permitted to depart, that faith receives, in place of the affections of the emotions, the communion of the Spirit. Then God reveals to us the fullness of His desire for our possessions and our fellowship with Him.

Look from the place where thou art

The place of separation becomes a place of vision. We may find ourselves in the midst of a struggle that we think will overcome us. When we yield to His mastery and are separate from all that would keep us from the heavenly vision, we shall find the valley of struggle to be the overlook upon a panorama of glory that is reserved for us.

The place of death becomes the place of life. For when we put to death an earthly affection, the life of God fills our souls and leads us on to possession with Him. We may think we are falling into a pit of despair if we allow some love to be cut from our life, but we will discover that from the pit we can see the stars.

Northward and southward and eastward and westward

When the separation is effected and we see the heavenly vision, we shall discover that the glory is to be found in every direction.

> Heaven above is softer blue,
> Earth around is sweeter green;
> Something lives in ev'ry hue
> Christless eyes have never seen.

The north is cold, the south is heat, the east is light, and the west is darkness, but when God opens our eyes, we see treasures in them all.

Life brings a cold disappointment or a warm delight: both will be used by us to bring us on toward God. We shall have light on some great problem, or walk in the darkness with our hand in His, and shall be content because He is there.

Verse 15: For all the land which thou seest, to thee will I give it

At first we have our possessions only by the promise of faith. The blessings of this life are ours at first even as heaven is ours now. We believe in it, and we know that some day it shall be ours in reality, but we do not know the joy of touching it and breathing its air. Thus it was with Abram at first. Even of that land he could say no more than

> There's a land that is fairer than day,
> And by faith we can see it afar.

But he had the promise of God that it belonged to him and he believed it, and that was the title deed. The actual occupancy came later.

Right now we have untold promises of God which we have not experienced. We accept them on His Word and we want to begin the possession. He will make good.

Verse 16: As the dust of the earth

Who can count the grains of the dust of this earth? So shall the physical descendants of Abraham be. For there is not yet mention of the heavenly seed that will be as the stars. God has a purpose for this earth, touched with the blood of His Son, and He will yet fulfill everything that He has spoken concerning it.

The earth may groan and travail together until now, waiting for the adoption (Romans 8:22), but the whole creation shall be delivered and Abraham's seed will be administrators of the blessing in God's time. When this nation that is now cast away, is once more received, it will mean life from the dead (Romans 11:15).

Verse 17: Arise, walk through the land . . . the length and the breadth of it

That which had been promised in Ur of the Chaldees, and had been seen from the borders, and now again from the place of separation, was to be possessed piecemeal. We know from the words of Moses to Israel (Deuteronomy 11:24), that the land was theirs in the measure of their occupation of it. It was all Abram's and his seed's by right and title, but when he had walked around an acre, he possessed an acre; when he had walked around a mile, he possessed a mile. When he climbed a hill, the hill was his, and when he descended into a valley, the valley was his.

So it is for us with all the promises of God. We are to possess the promises from Genesis to Revelation. Wherever we plant our feet in possession, the promises will become ours.

Verse 18: Abram dwelt in . . . Mamre . . . in Hebron

The names of the Bible always have meanings, and if they are studied carefully, there can be great blessing. When Abram first entered the land, he pitched his tent at Bethel, which means "house of God." He left that place for Egypt which became a "house of slaves." Now he was back, a more joyful and a wiser man. He has been uncompromising, and has fully obeyed the Lord by separating from his kindred.

He now dwells in Mamre, which means "vision," and pitches his tent in Hebron which comes from a verb meaning "joined together," hence "communion." At Bethel Abram had worshipped; at Hebron he knows true fellowship with God. Thus faith marches on to greater faith. As far as he knows, Abram is one with God, and the joy of the Lord is his.

Built there an altar unto the Lord

There was more at this altar than there was at the altar of Bethel. He knew God much better by now, and had learned the great lesson of Egypt. True love is always "more today than yesterday, and less today than tomorrow." Abram was learning this. "The path of the just is as the dawning light, that shineth more and more unto the perfect day" (Proverbs 4:18, ERV).

It is impossible to walk with God without acquiring greater knowledge of Him, and experiencing more wonderful communion with Him, for " . . . he who began a good work in you will bring it to completion at the day of Jesus Christ" (Philippians 1:6, RSV). The altars in Bethel and Hebron may have appeared alike to the casual observer, but the heart of Abram was now in communion.

Genesis 14

Verse 1: Amraphel

For years the critics of the Bible laughed at the fourteenth chapter of Genesis. The encyclopedias of a hundred years ago do not mention the existence of Amraphel. This chapter was named as "proof" against inspiration. And then the positive identification of Amraphel as Hammurabi was made. The code of laws which he set forth was discovered, and the chapter was proven historical.

Verse 2: These made war

This is the first recorded war in history. Wars come from the fallen state of man and from the lusts that war in the members of the human race (James 4:1). Even the most peaceful nation must learn the art of war in order to repel attackers. In this case, it should be noted that the four kings in the first verse are of the line of Shem, while the five kings in the second verse are of the line of Ham.

Lot had chosen Sodom, and was living among the accursed people. God is going to bring him out, even though it takes a war to do it. God will always order events to take care of His own, and to bring all His plans to fruition.

Verse 4: Twelve years they served

And they should have, for God pronounced the curse of servitude upon them, when Noah announced their destiny to Ham and Canaan. The conflict is about to touch Abram because his nephew, Lot, is dwelling in the midst of the kings of Ham. Their warfare against those who had been put over them by God Himself is about to involve Abram, in whom is the seed of promise.

There are three parties: the world, the flesh and the man of faith. The last must war against the two former, even while they are fighting each other.

Verses 5, 9: Rephaims, Zuzims, Emims . . . four kings with five

The Rephaim, the Zuzim and the Emim were the demon forces which produced giants in Noah's time and afterward. It is interesting to note that the religious world (the four kings), fights against the irreligious world (the five kings), and overcomes it; but the man of faith must not be deceived by the victory. The religious world may slay certain giants and have waves of reform, but the net result is always the same.

The carnal Christian (Lot) will always return to Sodom, and the spiritual man (Abram) will have to stand against all, for he stands alone with God. The moral victory of the religious world must not be confused with the spiritual victory of the man of faith.

Verse 12: Lot . . . dwelt in Sodom

In the beginning Lot merely pitched his tent toward Sodom (13:12). Now we find him dwelling within the city. The lust for good land had taken him into the neighborhood of sin, and the seductive power of the environment became too much for him. From the fellowship of Abram to a tent in the lush grass was only the first step. From the tent to the town was the second step. The remaining steps are inevitable. There is only one way of victory — complete separation.

They took Lot

Abram, dwelling at "vision" and "communion" (Mamre, Hebron) was absolutely untroubled by the wars and rumors of wars between the four kings and the five kings. They were of the deepest concern to Lot, because he was dwelling where he had no business to be. Lot will always be captured in such a warfare, simply because he is living in Sodom.

Verse 13: One . . . told Abram the Hebrew

The man who is truly separated unto God has the real power to help in the time of need. Though the world will not admit it, the presence of groups of surrendered, praying Christians is of more importance to our land than the possession of the atomic bomb. The enemy may have bombs, but he cannot duplicate righteous men, whose effectual, fervent prayers avail much (James 5:16).

The word Hebrew comes from a root that means "passed over." The Septuagint translates it "the passenger." Abram had passed over the Euphrates river; he was separated from Ur of the Chaldees, from his kindred and from his father's house, even as the Lord had commanded him (12:1). Now he was in position to prevail.

He dwelt in the plain of Mamre

He did not move till his fellow believer was in danger. The world wants to enlist the man of faith as an ally, but the true man of faith will not join the world in its efforts to subdue Sodom, nor will he join Sodom in its efforts to throw off the yoke of the world. Both sides will put up plausible arguments, but the man of faith has no place even in moral controversies that occupy much of the thought of the world.

The world cannot understand that the true pilgrim will not join in the fight on open evils; Christians like Lot will sometimes make common cause with the godless and unclean, in order to break the yoke of Sodom. Abram will dwell aloof, misunderstood by all but God.

Verse 14: When Abram heard that his brother was taken

The calm dignity of the man of faith is beautifully brought out here. He could have said, "It served him right"; or "He had it coming to him." But the man of God is a man of sympathy. He knows the inner meaning of "Judge not, that ye be not judged" (Matthew 7:1). Perhaps Abram remembered how he had been tempted to go to Egypt. He was a spiritual man and was restoring Lot in a spirit of meekness (Galatians 6:1).

The yielded believer cannot have within him a root of bitterness. There is nothing that marks a man as being like Christ more than his genuine love for someone who has been the cause of a deep wrong.

He armed

Only when a believer is enmeshed in the religious world does the pilgrim come down from the quiet hills of promise. Observe that Abram did not fight the moral evil of Sodom — in chapter 18 he prayed for the Sodomites. He does not fight the religious evil of the world, for they have captured a believer. It is always thus.

In His day, Christ our Lord pitied the publicans and harlots, and assailed and judged the Pharisees. The moral Pharisees called our Lord a glutton and a winebibbler (Matthew 11:19), a friend of publicans and sinners. This was because the religious, unsaved man can never understand the motives of the spiritual, born-again man. Wisdom is justified of her children.

Trained servants

Fortunately, Abram was not a pacifist. He lived in the midst of wars and rumors of wars and he took the precaution to train his servants. We do not know how many more servants he left at home with the cattle; but the 318 were given arms and pursued the enemy into his own territory. Abram, as the previous chapter clearly shows, was a man of peace, not moved by covetousness or ambition.

The man of faith is a realist, not a passive coward, or one incapable of leadership. When the crisis comes, he draws new strength from God and pursues to victory.

Verse 16: He brought back all

The preceding chapter shows us a meek and lowly Abram, yielding his rights to Lot. The present chapter shows us a courageous Abram, a man of decision and great ability, displaying initiative, tenacity and capacity. How does such a man suddenly display great gifts, unsuspected hitherto? The answer is that all his resources are in God.

The Holy Spirit came upon some to give them the gift of fine needlework (Exodus 28:39); upon others to give them the gift of jewelry; masonry and wood-working (Exodus 31:3-5). He came upon Joseph with the Holy Spirit of good administration (Genesis 41:38). Here we see Him giving Abram the gift of generalship and with it the victory.

Verse 17: Sodom went out to meet him

The world is not too much interested in praising the victory of a believer, but it is interested in getting back the booty. Shakespeare tells us that "sweet are the uses of adversity"; but we may add that the uses of prosperity are revealing. Kings now come out to meet the victor whose victory reveals him to be greater than his circumstances.

Some people would have had their heads turned by worldly recognition from a king. But not Abram. When John Knox was asked if he were frightened by the prospect of meeting the Queen of Scotland, he replied that he had just spent four hours with God. Such a man can't be much impressed by a mere king.

Verse 18: Melchizedek

This is the first mention of the greatest character of the Old Testament. We would consider Abram the greatest, if the New Testament did not tell us flatly that Melchizedek was the better (Hebrews 7:7). If you were reading the Bible for the first time you would soon pass by this figure who fills but three verses, jointly with Abram, and is not mentioned again until Psalm 110:4.

But the writer to the Hebrews devotes several chapters concerning Melchizedek and his role in the plan of God. We do not even know his name, for *melek* means "king" and *tsidek* means "righteousness" (as in Jeremiah 23:6). But he was a portrait of Christ, welcoming the pilgrim after the battle.

Sodom . . . Salem

There is a vast difference between corruption and peace, and a vast difference between their kings and what they stand for. Abram acknowledged his dependence upon the king of Salem, but declared his independence of the king of Sodom. He knew that he was inferior to Salem and paid tithes to him; he knew that he was superior to Sodom, and refused to be beholden to him. Before the king of Salem, he was humble and deferential; before the king of Sodom, he was firm and uncompromising.

Spiritual insight made him aware of the difference between the two men. One stood for God, the other for the lusts of the flesh. Abram knew, as though by instinct where there was power and where there was peril.

King of Salem

This is the second of his titles. He is the perfect type of the priesthood of Christ (Psalm 110:4), since he is the symbol of eternity. He comes from somewhere, disappears into somewhere, but, purposely, God does not record his ancestry or his posterity (Hebrews 7:3, 6). After the battle with the four kings, God sends the priest of righteousness and peace to crowd Abram with fellowship and to bring him into a new relationship with Himself. When Abram was faithful, God revealed Himself still more to him.

Bread and Wine

Bread is the symbol of life (John 6:50), wine the symbol of joy (Psalm 104:15). These are the accompaniments of righteousness and peace. And when they are given by the One who is both King of righteousness and King of peace, they are given in royal fashion. A king can do no less. The King came that we might have life and that we might have it more abundantly (John 10:10), and spoke to us that our joy might be full (John 15:11).

We know these symbols, of course, as those of the body and blood of our Lord, and we feed upon them in the communion service. Our communion with Him is because of the giving of His body and the pouring out of His blood by which we live and joy in Him.

Priest

The King is revealed to be a priest. This is highly significant, for throughout the long period from Moses to Christ, priests were forbidden to reign and kings were forbidden to exercise the functions of the priest. The absolute separation of religion and the state is a mighty Biblical principle. Only one is capable of being both priest and king, the Lord Jesus Christ, and He has chosen us to be kings and priests before Him (I Peter 2:9).

Most high God

This name for God is remarkable because it occurs four times in this paragraph, its first use in the Scripture. The Hebrew *El Elyon* means "The Highest God." All the gods of the nations are idols, and behind these idols are demons; but our God is the Being who is supreme.

It is significant that God was known to this Gentile king by this name. Through the years, from Noah, through Shem, this knowledge of the true God had been preserved by Him for this moment. Abram was to be blessed by this priest, who was not of Aaron's priesthood, but who was a picture of the eternal priesthood of the Lord Jesus.

Verse 19: He blessed him

When we are empty, we need to be filled. At the end of a day of battle, the Lord comes with His provision. Filled with the bread and the wine of God, the soul wants nothing more. The men of faith may be met by the rulers of this world's darkness when the conflict is over, but the bread and wine of the King of righteousness and peace so fills them that they turn away from food that the world offers.

"If He is thy God, if thus He meets thee by His priest, in an hour of weakness feasting thee with bread and wine, for which others have labored, and which cost thee nothing, then thou needest not the gifts of Sodom's fallen king."

Possessor of heaven and earth

The supreme God rules over all. This, significantly enough, is the title to which Lucifer aspired. He did not say, I will ascend . . . I will be like the Redeemer. For to be the Redeemer it was necessary for the Lord Jesus to go down (Philippians 2:6-8). But in saying, "I will ascend . . . I will make myself like the most High" (Isaiah 14:13, 14), Lucifer showed his pride and his greed.

Verse 20: And blessed be the most high God

It is striking to see this solitary figure, the king of Salem, standing between Abram and God, bringing down a stream of blessing upon Abram and sending up a stream of worship.

The downward blessing is a blessing of deeds — God touches us with provision of life and joy. We cannot give anything to God, so that when we bless Him, we pour up to Him the acknowledgment of His praise. His being requires the acknowledgement of His worth, and that is worth-ship, worship.

The Lord told the woman at the well that the Father seeks true worshipers who will worship Him in Spirit and in truth.

101

It is almost pathetic that God has to hunt out among believers, those who will do what He wants.

And he gave Him tithes of all

The victor became a giver. The importance of this is set forth in Hebrews where we are told that Abraham's great-grandson, Levi, was in Abraham's loins when he bowed down before Melchizedek, and that this demonstrates the superiority of the heavenly eternal priesthood of Christ over the earthly, temporary priesthood of Aaron (Hebrews 7:9, 10).

It is a great illustration of the fact that we may involve our great-grandchildren by some act of ours, and it had better be an involvement for blessing than for a curse. The revelation of God as the most High struck through to Abram's being, for from then on he found his only good in Him, and refused to be enriched from any other quarter.

The New Testament says of Melchizedek, "See how great he is! Abraham the patriarch gave him a tithe of the spoils" (Hebrews 7:4). If Abram had given the king a present, we would have understood it as a gesture of courtesy between equals. But Abram took quite a different attitude. He did not stand before Salem as an equal, but took the place of submission at once. The fact that he gave tithes is the acknowledgment of duty. Melchizedek came as the minister of God, performing a duty. He stood between the most High and Abram as a mediator, and thus Abram had a duty to perform toward him. The present would have been given to a king as a friend; the tithes are paid to the representative of God.

Verse 21: Give me the persons . . . take the goods

All belonged to Abram by right of conquest, for the king of Sodom had lost it in battle. But he now wants his subjects back, and is willing to compromise to get as much as he can. He asks for the captives and is willing to let Abram take the goods. Here is another temptation great as those which had gone before.

The worldly king is offering a fellowship that would be understood by all as participation with him in all that was possessed. But Abram has eaten the bread and drunk the wine which Melchizedek has given him, and strong in that strength he resists.

102

Verse 22: I have lift up my hand unto the Lord, the most high God

This is the third revelation of God which Abram has received. At Ur it was the God of glory who appeared unto him (Acts 7:2). When Abram reached Bethel, God appeared unto him as Jehovah, and he built an altar to Him there (Genesis 12:8).

Even though the Lord did not reveal all that was in that name of redemption, it was a great advance in the knowledge of God. But now God appears to Abram as *El Elyon,* most High God, possessor of heaven and earth. With every succeeding need there was a new revelation of God, and a new entrance by faith into the knowledge of Him. Abram makes an agreement, a vow. He will be possessed by the Possessor.

Verse 23: I will not take from a thread . . . a shoelatchet

If God is most High, possessor of heaven and earth, He is able to take care of His servants; and Abram who has seen His glory and followed Him from Ur, is not going to compromise by taking strings and sandal-thongs from a Sodomite king. For if he had done so, the Sodomite would have claimed a part of his glory forever.

If the world can claim part of the success of a child of God, then the sting is taken from the witness. But if all the glory is given to God, then the world cannot take any part of it, and the believer becomes, as Paul says, " . . . as having nothing, and yet possessing everything" (II Corinthians 6:9, 10).

Lest thou shouldest say, I have made Abram rich

When the uncompromising stand is taken, the soul is thrown back on God. Abram had strengthened his own faith by announcing that it was all in God, and all blessings were from God. Now he would not be tempted to come down into Sodom for any favor.

Ezra did the same thing, and when he was in difficulty, his stand forced him back on God. He said, "For I was ashamed to ask the king for a band of soldiers and horsemen to protect us against the enemy on our way; since we had told the king, 'The hand of our God is for good' . . . So we fasted and besought our God for this" (Ezra 8:22, 23, RSV).

Verse 24: The young men . . . which went with me

Abram did not try to make his companions live up to his standards. He was going to live by faith, trusting utterly in the Lord, but Aner, Eshcol and Mamre were not spiritually advanced enough to do this. They were to get their portion of the booty. Abram's portion was the Lord.

Older Christians should never seek to force younger Christians to live according to advanced standards of which the younger ones have no personal experience. It is vain to set up standards for babes in Christ which only a mature Christian can know from the daily supplies of grace which God gives. If Abram had insisted that the young Canaanites refuse the booty, they might have gone away without it in their hands, but they would have had the lust for it in their hearts.

Genesis 15

Verse 1: After these things

Every day and every hour is a new beginning with God. After failure we can begin afresh with Him. After success we need to begin with Him. It makes no difference what the past has contained of failure or success, the present and future are all with which we need be concerned. The principle of "forgetting what lies behind" (Philippians 3:13) is a divine principle, and every new beginning with God will lead to higher ground of power and privilege.

Abram had won a strategic spiritual and an economic victory. The kings had been defeated, Melchizedek had given him a blessing and Abram had refused material wealth from man. Therefore, he is in special need, and God is the One who supplies all our need. It is noteworthy that Christ spent all night in prayer after His greatest triumphs.

The word of the Lord came

God's method of supplying our need is to give us fresh knowledge of Himself, for every need can be met by seeing Him. This is the first time that the well-known phrase, oft repeated in the Bible, is to be found — the Word of the Lord came. The Word of the Lord came in many and various ways (Hebrews 1:1), but the Word always had its effect. That is why Christ said, "Sanctify them in the truth; thy word is truth" (John 17:17, RSV). The Word of the Lord is living and powerful (Hebrews 4:12) and will always produce the effect that God has determined for it (Isaiah 55:11). The Lord of the Word gives Himself in His Word, and that is the answer to our need.

105

Fear not, Abram

Fear is a natural part of the make-up of the human race. Cowards are afraid before a battle; heroes are afraid afterward. Abram had the natural reaction to the great events of the last chapter. For a peaceful old man to go into battle against four powerful kings was a great experience, and when the crisis was over, the strain of body, mind and spirit began to show. At such a time, God comes with His comforting word, "Fear not."

This is the first use of this phrase in the Word. It, and "Be not afraid," occurs well over a hundred times in Scripture.

I am thy shield

The man who administers a defeat to the world becomes a target for its hatred. Abram had left his sheltered hills to rescue his nephew, Lot. The four kings who were powerful enough to defeat the five kings were in turn beaten by Abram plus God. They certainly had the resources to regroup and come against him with superior forces. But at this point God reveals to Abram that He is his ally, and therefore his shield.

There need be no fear of the power of the world against us, if we remain in the center of the Lord's will. No weapon that is formed against us shall prosper (Isaiah 54:17). We may be strong in the Lord and in the power of His might.

The Lord always provides the armor for His people, and that armor is Himself. Even Satan confessed to God that when he tried to get Job, he had been turned back by the hedge which God had placed around him (Job 1:10). The whole armor of God (Ephesians 6:11) has been provided, and our enemies must break through God Himself to reach us. "For you have died, and your life is hid with Christ in God" (Colossians 3:3, RSV). He is around us as a "wall of fire" (Zechariah 2:5). The believer may laugh at his enemies when he knows where he is in God.

Thy exceeding great reward

No man ever lost anything by giving up something for God. The Lord has never remained in debt to any man. Abram had refused to take anything from a thread to a sandal-thong lest the king of Sodom should boast that he had contributed to the prosperity of God's man.

106

The Lord comes to those who put their trust in Him thus, and provides for all their need according to His riches (the principal) with glory (the interest) by Christ Jesus (the payment). That promise to the Philippians (4:19) was given by God to Abram as encouragement for us. When we look above the blessing to the One who blesses, we have learned the simple mathematical rule that the whole is greater than any of its parts.

Verse 2: And Abram said, Lord God

Faith immediately answers to the Word of God, for faith comes by hearing and hearing by the Word of God (Romans 10:17). God has said that " . . . the path of the righteous is like the light of dawn, which shines brighter and brighter until full day" (Proverbs 4:18, RSV). This is true because of the chain reaction and interaction of faith and the Word of God.

God reveals Himself and faith lays hold upon the revelation and feeds upon it. Thus faith grows and turns itself back to God, who then gives a further revelation of Himself, so that faith has more upon which to feed and grow. There were nine different manifestations of God to Abram, of which this is the fifth.

What wilt thou give me?

A human being is a frail creature. Even faith is contaminated when it touches the human heart. God had just told Abram not to fear, and had promised to be his shield and his reward. He had promised to be his great reward. And yet Abram answers with almost a plaintive cry. The strain of the preceding day's conflict, the long march with his little army, the reaction of victory and renunciation were all very great.

Seeing I go childless

Ten years had elapsed since Abram arrived in the land. The promise of his being made a great nation was becoming dim. He was old and lonely. Both he and Sarah were beyond the age of child-bearing. To all outward appearances his heir was a servant who had been born in his house and was now his steward.

The prospect was not encouraging and Abram spreads it before the Lord. Even when we have the promise and are

107

unwilling to wait for its fulfillment, He is kind to us, and goes along with us in our weakness.

Verse 3: Me Thou hast given no seed

As a matter of fact God had given Abram seed as the stars of the sky and the sands of the sea. The Word of God was far more than a birth certificate, but Abram had not fully realized it.

A promise from God to pay is more than money in the hand from anyone else. During World War II our government officials told us that if we would invest three dollars in bonds, we would get back four in ten years. They didn't tell us that the mounting price spiral would reduce the four dollars to $1.98 or less. There is no inflation or deflation with God's promises. His Word is His bond, and the word "bond" implies a chain. He is bound to fulfill that which His Word has spoken.

Verse 4: This shall not be thine heir

God did not chide Abram for his lack of faith, for He saw that there was some faith, and proceeded to feed and cultivate that faith. The verse begins, "And, behold, the word of the Lord came to him." It was a word of correction, and one that reveals the tender heart of God.

Why does a mother tell a child a hundred times not to do something? Simply because ninety-nine times is not enough. "Love is patient and kind" (I Corinthians 13:4). God's love is the longest suffering and the kindest. The Word of the Lord is "profitable for . . . correction" (II Timothy 3:16), and that was what the Lord was now doing in Abram.

He that shall come forth out of thine own bowels

God is a God of encouragement. He knows our frame and remembers that we are dust (Psalm 103:14). He knows that we live in a world of illusion with senses that have been dulled by sin and are subject to the mirages of this world's murky light. So He comes to us when we are inclined to faint and comforts us with the absolute promise of His Word in terms that cannot be misinterpreted.

Job saw God through the worms of decomposition and decay (Job 19:26). Abram now feels God in the tightening of his own bowels. Since he is the father of all who believe (Romans 4:11),

108

and since these things were written for us and not for him only (Romans 4:23), we grasp the promise, lay it on the ground and stand on it.

Verse 5: And He brought him forth abroad

Had Abram been living within himself? At all events he was away from the light, the air and the stars. But God brought him forth. God is always at work in His children and He expects to bless them, therefore He brings them to where they can see the blessing before they touch it.

God can bring us out, even if it takes a war, the capture of Lot and the abandoning of property. Then we will see the stars, beyond the stars the promises, and beyond the promises God Himself.

Look . . . and tell the stars

It was not merely the absence of an heir to his fortune that troubled Abram; it was the absence of the heir that would bring the line of the Messiah. For Abram was beginning to see Christ's day (John 8:56), which undoubtedly means that he was receiving an ever growing revelation of the scheme and scope of salvation by Christ's coming to die for us, and he had seen the extension of the Church throughout the Gentile world. He was impatient for all this to begin.

So now God affirms and confirms the promise. The stars surpass the eyes of man, whether they be the physical eyes or the giant telescopes which peer into the nearer edges of God's space.

So shall thy seed be

God took particular pains to tell Abram that his descendants would be an innumerable company. First, He told him that they would be as the dust of the earth (13:16). Here He tells him that they shall be as the stars of heaven (15:5). Later, He tells him that they shall be as the sand upon the seashore (22:17). I do not believe that we can understand all that this means. Israel and the church: certainly.

Verse 6: And he believed in the Lord

This is the first mention of belief in the Bible. We know that there was faith before Abram, for God tells us of the faith of Abel, of Enoch and of Noah (Hebrews 11:4, 5, 7). But now

God sets it down. The reason is that the faith of Abram was the first full-orbed faith that comprehended Christ and His day. It must be this or else the statements that his faith was the same as ours (Romans 4:12, 16) would not be true. There was more than a mere belief in God's power; there was faith that went through to the Messiah and was based on Him.

He counted it to him

This is the first mention of justification in the Bible. Whatever translation is used, the meaning is the same. He "imputed" it; He "reckoned it"; He "credited" it. It was all God's doing. He is the keeper of the eternal records. He is the Judge before whom all cases are tried. He is the One who condemns or justifies. And these two words — "condemn" and "justify" — are opposites. No one who is condemned has been justified, and no one who has been justified can be condemned (Romans 8:1).

For righteousness

This is the first mention of righteousness in the Bible, but the idea has been on every page and in every line. The main subject of the Bible is "righteousness." The Bible is the story of the One who is righteousness, of Lucifer who lost righteousness; of how God judged the world in righteousness; and planned for man and the manifestation of righteousness in Christ; how He bought righteousness through the shedding of blood; of the way Christ was made righteousness unto all believers; and of the ultimate triumph of righteousness in all the creation.

Abram's faith was counted unto him — not merely instead of righteousness, but *for* righteousness; with the purpose of making a way whereby he could receive imputed righteousness.

Verse 7: And He said unto him, I am the Lord

This is one further step, and therefore one further revelation of the nature and being of God. God's continual revelation of Himself is the only way to grow in grace and in knowledge of Himself.

I brought thee out of Ur . . . to give thee this land

Abram had become discouraged and thought it was time for God to act. But God's delays are never denials. He gives us a promise and wishes us to grow in that promise. When we

110

have learned the first lesson, He will teach us the second. He never attempts to teach algebra to the one who has not learned the multiplication table.

Fifteen years more went by before Isaac was born, but now Abram was resting in faith, and God reminds him that He is working with a definite purpose. Abram was not brought out to wander, but to settle, and while he would never know the land in peace, and there would be the ebb and flow of events and centuries, yet the promise was sure, and the deed for his inheritance was sure.

Verse 8: Whereby shall I know

This question came not from idle curiosity, but from a heart of faith. It is interesting to note that Zacharias asked the same question when he was told that he would become the father of John the Baptist. "How shall I know this?" (Luke 1:18), and he was struck dumb for his unbelieving query.

But Abram was asking to be more clearly informed. The question is consistent with the strongest faith, and God was quick to answer with details and a guarantee which was as strong as the Godhead. Abram's motive was a high one, that of Zacharias was a low one. That is why Abram received a gracious answer, Zacharias a sharp rebuke.

Abram was asking for a sign from God. In many instances throughout the Bible, God answers the honest questions of His people and condescends in grace to give them a material sign. He knows our frame and remembers that we are dust (Psalm 103:14). Therefore it is not wrong for Gideon to put out a fleece or for Hezekiah to ask for a movement of the shadow on the dial (Judges 6:36-40; II Kings 20:8-11).

A question that comes from a heart that is trusting God is good and acceptable to Him. He can discern between the honest and the frivolous question. He tells a curious Peter that it is none of his business how John is to die (John 21:22), but he commends the faith of Abram and answers his inquiries.

Verse 9: Take Me an heifer

This is one of the strangest answers ever given to a question. Yet, it was the only possible answer. "How am I to know that I shall possess it?" "Bring Me a heifer." One might think that the dial of the radio had slipped from one program to another.

111

The question is asked on a program of legal advice. The answer comes from a broadcast of the department of agriculture.

But the heifer and the inheritance are bound together in the mind of God. The heifer is to be killed and its blood is to be shed. The Lord is saying that the guarantee of the title of the land to Israel is nothing short of the cross of Jesus Christ. All God's promises are Yea and Amen in Christ (II Corinthians 1:20), and the promise of the land to Israel is guaranteed by this symbol of the cross of Christ.

Three years old

Abram was to bring only fully mature animals. Each animal must have attained the perfection of maturity, for nothing but a perfect sacrifice could be used for the ratification of God's covenant with man. All clean animals for sacrifice, later indicated to Moses in the law to be used in the sacrifices before the Lord, were now required of Abram. The dove and pigeon were included because the sacrifices must be within the reach of all. The rich might bring an heifer, and the poor, who would not possess so much, could bring a pigeon.

Verse 10: He . . . divided them in the midst

In our courts men are asked to take oath upon a Bible; in the courts of Islam men swear by the beard of the prophet Mohammed. This dividing the bodies of animals was a most solemn method of taking an oath, as both Greek and Roman authors state.

The parties to the oath walked around the two heaps of flesh in the path of a figure eight. God judges the men who broke the covenant after having cut the calf in two, and passed between its parts (Jeremiah 34:18, 19). They had chiseled by offering a calf — not a three-year old — and had broken their covenant. Here God is telling Abram to prepare the properties for the solemn taking of an oath.

Verse 11: The fowls came down

The Lord began to teach Abram that the land would be occupied against much opposition. Birds, in the Scriptures, are often a symbol of enemies. Joseph told the baker that birds were to eat his flesh (Genesis 40:19). The tree that harbored fowls in Nebuchadnezzar's vision was ordered hewn down by

112

God (Daniel 4:12-14); the fowls snatched away the seed that was sown on the hard ground (Matthew 13:4).

The prophecy has been verified in many ways. Egypt sought to keep Israel from the land; the birds of Canaan made them a prey. Birds of Greece and Rome and of Islam have cawed against the Jews, and today the Arabs oppose their possession of Palestine.

Abram drove them away

Israel has had to contend for the land and Abram's fight with the birds is still going on. But faith lays hold upon the promises of God and is willing to fight till death for the cause that has been ordered and guaranteed by Him. Time and again in the days of the Judges, the Samsons and the Gideons drove off the birds. For seventy years of the captivity, the birds of Babylon roosted and hovered over Israel, and then came many another flock. Jews died by the hundreds of thousands to defend Jerusalem in the days of Titus.

All this was shown to Abram in the pageant which God set before him. The believer will never be frightened by difficulties when he knows that God has given him the inheritance.

Verse 12: When the sun was going down

In verse five God brought Abram out under the canopy of stars — it was the night of the promise. The question was asked and the Lord kept Abram occupied with the pageant through the day, and now the sun is going down on a night of conflict and trouble. "Darkness is as light with thee" (Psalm 139:12).

The slowness of the fulfillment of the promise is set forth in this long passage of time, but the delay is not a denial, and the sun will rise again upon the land and upon Abram's seed in the land. For "Light rises in the darkness for the upright; the Lord is gracious, merciful and righteous" (Psalm 112:4, RSV).

A deep sleep

Several times in the Bible, God tells us of deep sleep falling upon someone. The first case was that of Adam, when the Lord took Eve from his side (Genesis 2:21). At times it was the deep sleep of judgment as when God caused Saul and his men to slumber so that David might seize the king's spear (I Samuel 26:12).

But the sleep that God gave Abram was like that which He twice gave Daniel (8:18; 10:9). Consciousness had to be barred in order that his being might lay hold upon the eternal things. In our day God does not work by visions and dreams, for we have the Book before us. But there is a sense in which we must close our eyes to the distractions around us and see God alone.

Horror

Here Abram was given a glimpse of that which His Lord would suffer when He came to earth. As Christ faced being made sin for us, there came upon Him an agony which caused Him to break into the bloody sweat of Gethsemane. After He had been on the cross for three hours, a great darkness fell upon the earth (Matthew 27:45), at the end of which the Lord Jesus cried, "My God, my God, why hast thou forsaken me?"

Any man who is to receive the covenant of God, like Abram, must enter into its knowledge through the shedding of blood, and the comprehension of what Christ has done. "Light rises in the darkness for the upright" (Psalm 112:4), and "In thy light do we see light" (Psalm 36:9).

Great darkness

The life of a believer has alternate periods of light and darkness. Even while watching beside the sacrifice, Abram felt the darkness that came down over the place of the shedding of the blood of the covenant. In Abram's sleep and darkness, he received a vision of the cross and of world history to the end of the age. Thus the hour of trial proved to be an hour of light.

Frequently fever, suffering and delirium leave a patient with a mind that is clear, and unimportant things are relegated to their unimportant place. We need never fear entering into unconsciousness and darkness with our Lord, for He always brings such trials upon us *beside the altar,* and thus we better understand the Lord Jesus Christ. The Psalmist could not understand the apparent injustice of life till he went into the sanctuary (Psalm 73:17).

Verse 13: Know of a surety

God never wants His children to know a thing half-way. He has made provision for us to know with surety. "Surely the Lord does nothing, without revealing his secret to his servants

114

the prophets" (Amos 3:7, RSV). Anyone who has a vague hope-so faith does not know the reality of God's revealed truth.

John tells us that "we know that the Son of God has come, and has given us understanding, to know . . . " (I John 5:20, RSV). That not only tells us that we know, but that we may know that we know. This certainty gives peace to the mind, and is diffused through our being. Note that this assurance of God is in answer to Abram's question, "How am I to know?" (verse 8). God points to the sacrifice and says, "Know of a surety."

A land that is not theirs

When will we learn that this is God's perfect description of the world in which His redeemed live? If we can only lay hold of this truth by faith and realize that believers have been created for heaven. Here on earth we are only as strangers in a land whose spirit and desire is alien to the Christ whom it crucified.

Thy seed . . . shall serve them

The world hated Christ before it ever hated a believer (John 15:18). The world is absolutely alien to God and spiritual things. Anything that a Christian has to do in this world is under a taskmaster who does not comprehend spiritual things. We live in the world of business, politics, society, even religion, all of which are dominated by thoughts that are contrary to our God. "They are surprised that you do not now join them in the same wild profligacy" (I Peter 4:4, RSV), and they never can think anything else.

Even though we work for a system that does not understand us, we have joy in our hearts because all that we do, even when serving a crooked master (I Peter 2:18), is done as unto the Lord and not unto men (Colossians 3:23). The believer serves the Lord even when the world is paying his wages.

They shall afflict them

Abram now learns that he is not to see the glorious fulfillment of the promises which have been made to him, but that he is to go on by faith, not seeing anything but the promise itself. Abram's children were to go through terrible affliction. They were to learn that "through much tribulation" they come into the Lord's kingdom. The affliction would be so terrible that even the soul of God would be grieved for the misery of Israel (Judges 10:16).

When we know that in all our afflictions He is Himself afflicted (Isaiah 63:9), anything becomes easy to take. We know that our Father permits it to come upon us and that He has even planned it.

Four hundred years

God's ways are not our ways (Isaiah 55:8). We are impatient because we are creatures of time. God is eternal and moves above our way of thinking and being.

A man who wants to raise mushrooms can get a crop overnight, but he must work in a dark cellar. A man who wants great oak trees will have them for his grandchildren but not for himself; but while he plants them and watches them develop slowly, he will be under the open sky.

A man of ninety who is told that his seed is to be the dust, the sand and the stars must learn the perspective of the plan of God. Before the accomplishment of the promise, there will be slavery, affliction, judgment and deliverance. Four centuries would pass (actually 430 years), but the Word of God would be fulfilled.

Verse 14: That nation . . . will I judge

Egypt may hold sway for a thousand years, and may leave behind her the weight of her pyramids and the mystery of her desert temples, but she has been judged by God, and she will be judged. "I will break the arms of Pharaoh," God declares (Ezekiel 30:24).

There is in the British Museum, the giant forearm of a god, fifteen feet long, with a fist three feet through. Its destruction attests the power of God to accomplish the judgment that He promised. The Egypt in which we live — the world — in which the believers are groaning, will be judged completely. God has spoken it.

They shall come out with great substance

Believers may be despised and rejected of men even as was our Lord (Isaiah 53:3), but we shall leave this world with great substance. It will not be with the silver and gold of this world, but with all that we have accomplished in the name of the risen Lord Jesus Christ, to take a spoil and a prey by laying up for ourselves treasures in heaven.

We shall carry out of this world the treasure of souls that we have won from the kingdom of the enemy, and the stores of grace that we have found by being patient in tribulation, loving under oppression and confident when promises seemed delayed. The Lord Jesus Christ disarmed the principalities and powers (Colossians 2:15), and we are "the strong" with whom He divides the spoil (Isaiah 53:12).

Verse 15: Thou shalt go . . . in peace

Abram was now convinced that the Lord was true and that His promises were certain, even though he, himself, would not see their accomplishment. He rested in the Word of God alone, and he needed no other guarantee. This was enough; this was peace. He was justified, and his path would shine more and more unto the perfect day (Proverbs 4:18).

To thy fathers

Terah and Abram's other ancestors were not buried in Canaan, but in Haran and in Ur of the Chaldees. This promise does not mean, therefore, that Abram was to be buried in the same plot with them, but that he would rejoin them in the land of the dead, awaiting the day when Christ would descend to release them and take them to be with Himself forever.

This is the first of many references which gives to all believers the comfort of knowing that we shall be with our loved ones after death, that we shall know them and be joined to the Lord *together with them*. It is to this phrase, meaningless without the certainty of our knowing our loved ones, that the Lord adds the commandment of comfort. "Together with them . . . comfort one another with these words" (I Thessalonians 4:17, 18).

In a good old age

The devil has no nice old people. Those who do not have the life of God within them grow meaner and more cantankerous as the years go by, and as they come nearer and nearer to eternal judgment. But "the trees of the Lord are watered abundantly" (Psalm 104:16, RSV), and the believer can grow old gracefully.

A good old age is that time of life in which the Christian,

117

knowing that the world looks upon him as a has-been, begins to see himself as one who is just beginning eternity. We do not enter eternal life when we die, but eternal life enters us when we are born again. When we've been there ten million years, bright shining as the sun, our life in heaven will be the same life that the Lord planted within us when we became partakers of the divine nature (II Peter 1:4).

Old age brings with it a thousand messengers that tell us that we are to leave our bodies. The wrinkles, the dimming eyesight, the creaking joints, the graying hair and all the rest of God's sweet messengers, call us from attachment to the flesh and help us turn our gaze upon the invisible and the eternal.

Verse 16: Iniquity . . . not yet full

If God asks us to be patient and to take the long view beyond generations and into centuries, it is because He is revealing to us that He is patient beyond comparison. We must never forget that God is engaged in the invisible war with the rebel prince, and that He is teaching eternal things to the few who will believe Him in the midst of a world of illusion and delusion.

We may look out upon a world that produces Hitlers and Stalins, and, seeing the horrors of their prison camps, cry out to God, "How long, O Lord" (Revelation 6:10), and the Lord answers that their iniquity is not yet full, that the number of martyrs is not yet fulfilled (Revelation 6:11), and bids us to wait. If the iniquity of the world had been full a hundred years ago, none of us would have been born to be born again.

Verse 17: When the sun went down

Since God began this experience with Abram while it was dark and the stars were shining (verse 5), we can see that he had been occupied with all these things for many long hours. From before dawn until after sunset, Abram had to wait in the heat of the day. Though much of the time was spent in preparing the sacrifices, also much time was spent in driving away the fowls (verse 11), and in sleep and the horror that came upon him (verse 12).

But after the long morning and the long afternoon of life, God gives some of His most wonderful blessings. As we grow older in the faith, its richest blessings come to us and the true meaning of the covenant of God grows upon us.

118

A smoking furnace

This is the first symbol of God's presence. Thus He appeared to Moses on Mount Sinai (Exodus 19:18). The furnace was well-known to ancient peoples; it was the small apparatus with which the silversmiths and goldsmiths melted down precious ores so that the dross could be drawn off, leaving the refined and pure elements.

The trial of our faith is much more precious than gold which perishes, though it be tried in the fire (I Peter 1:7).

The Lord is with His own in the furnace (Daniel 3:25). The smith who thus purifies the metal keeps the fire burning until the dross comes to the top. He removes this until the molten metal is clear enough to reflect his own face. Thus the Lord sits as a refiner and purifier of silver (Malachi 3:3), and the furnace will burn until He sees His image in us.

A burning lamp

In God's dealings with His children, the long day of trial ends with light. The believer recognizes his own nothingness and turns utterly to the Lord, knowing himself to be sterile and barren. Then the Lord turns on the light, Himself, since God is light and in Him dwells no darkness at all (I John 1:5).

God appeared to Moses in a burning bush (Exodus 3:2), and in a burning mountain to Israel (Exodus 19:18, Hebrews 12:18); he led them through the wilderness as a pillar of smoke and fire by night, and of cloud by day (Exodus 14:19, 20; 24:17). He tells us later (Isaiah 4:5), that this was for a glory and a defense for His people.

Verse 18: In the same day

All of this: the blood sacrifice, the oath of God, the smoking furnace and the flaming torch symbolized the Lord Jesus Christ. When our Lord tells us that Abram rejoiced to see His day, and was glad (John 8:56), we may well believe that at this sunset Christ's day increased its light for Abram. God has no blessings for any man apart from the work of Christ. In the day of Calvary, all the promises are seen, and in the dawn of that sunset, after we see the darkness of God on Calvary, we shall be lightened forever more. When we see His day, we shall rejoice and be glad.

119

The Lord made a covenant

The Lord did it all; Abram did nothing. The Lord passed between the burning pieces of the sacrifice, but Abram did not. If men had been making a mutual covenant, both parties would have moved in the figure eight among the pieces, but here God moves alone.

The covenants of God are not agreements between two parties; the promises of God begin and end with Himself. They are unilateral agreements, divinely and blessedly one-sided. God promises, God blesses, God gives, God guarantees, God assures, and since He "desired to show more convincingly to the heirs of the promise the unchangeable character of his purpose" (Hebrews 6:17, RSV), He confirms it by oath.

Have I given this land

The promises of God are sure, and are all in the past tense as far as He is concerned. What, then, is the part of man in these covenants of God? Unquestionably our part is to receive all that God gives in grace. David asks, "What shall I render to the Lord for all his bounty to me?" (Psalm 116:12, RSV). It is the same question we have asked. And listen to his answer: "I will lift up the cup of salvation and call on the name of the Lord" (v. 13, RSV). What shall I give? God says, "I'll do the giving. You take."

The old word "render" means to give, and the French form, with the reflexive for self *se rendre,* has given us "surrender." To a God who does everything we must say, "Here, Lord, I give myself away: 'Tis all that I can do."

From the river . . . unto the river

To deny that the children of Israel will literally possess Palestine, far beyond anything they have ever touched, becomes unbelief that is effrontery. God has something for literal Israel. Once we were Gentiles, dogs that took the crumbs from Israel's table (Mark 7:28).

Let us never hold that all the blessings are now for the Church, and refuse even the crumbs of earthly promises to the Israel whom God has chosen to possess the land for His glory. God has told us to pray for the peace of Jerusalem, and that they who love those walls shall prosper (Psalm 122:6).

Verse 20: . . . the Hittites . . .

The amazing scope of the promise to Israel now becomes evident. The Hittites were the descendants of Ham, and were under a curse. For centuries this great power would fight against Israel; these mighty cousins of the Egyptians and Canaanites would contest the provisions of this deed and its title insurance of Calvary. But they would one day be blotted out, and this has happened. Just as surely their land — and note that their great country was what is now Asia Minor — must one day come under the rule of God's people, chosen to be the colonial administrators of the earth in that day when the Lord redeems His promises which were made to earthly peoples.

Genesis 16

Verse 1: Sarai Abram's wife bare him no children

A promise made to Abram was also a promise to Sarai, for a man's wife is one with him in the sight of God. Sarai was to Abram as Eve was to Adam, and as the true Church is to the Lord Jesus Christ.

The natural desires of the human heart are to be, to appear, to seem, to possess, and this not only for ourselves but for the posterity we beget in our own image. The lesson that God is about to teach concerning Sarai, we are directly told in the New Testament, is an allegory concerning our faith (Galatians 4:24).

Abram was justified by faith, but this did not keep him from trying to do something in his own strength. God is seeking to bring us to realize our utter nothingness, in order that we may utterly depend upon Him. Abram believed God, but he was looking to himself and Sarai to fulfill the promise. He would turn and look to Hagar. He had to learn to look to God.

Verse 2: The Lord hath restrained me fom bearing

Sarai saw the result of the Lord's restraint, but she did not know the reason. Her motives were probably good, for she knew the promise to Abram and was impatient for its fulfillment. It had not yet been revealed that she was to be the mother.

In her impatience, she was trying to help God to do something by human means. She did not comprehend that sterility and barrenness in the Christian life are used by God to put us on our faces before Him that we may bring forth fruit, more

122

fruit, much fruit, and fruit that remains, even as Christ said (John 15:1-8). The first temptation that comes with the knowledge of barrenness is always that we must do something about it in human strength. This hope, too, must be destroyed if we are to be truly fruitful.

Go in unto my maid

The dear old woman wanted so much to see the promise accomplished, but the proposal was wrong in every way. W. H. Griffith Thomas has pointed out that this action "was wrong against God, whose word had been given and whose time should have been waited. It was wrong against Abraham, leading him out of the pathway of patient waiting for God's will. It was wrong against Hagar, and did not recognize her individuality and rights in the matter. It was wrong against Sarai herself, robbing her of a high privilege as well as leading to disobedience." And I may add that it was wrong against the child who was born of this union, for he became a "wild-ass man." God said that Ishmael could never be the heir.

I may obtain . . . by her

The flesh will do anything except die to obtain by God. It must have been galling to Sarai to know that she was barren. Now she succumbs to the great temptation to follow the ancient custom according to which the child of a slave was counted the child of the mistress.

Since God tells us in Galatians that Hagar represents the law and Sarai grace, this story illustrates the false idea that grace can obtain something by legalistic means. The human heart hates pure grace, and man yearns to do something for God. Law seeks to obtain by doing, grace accepts all freely.

Abram hearkened

The temptation to Abram originated in Sarai. Of course, Abram should not have yielded. After the wonders of the night of the stars, the day of the sacrifice and the evening of the covenant, Abram should have been impervious to such a temptation. No perfect feet walk the path of faith. We go forward as a baby learns to walk — the right foot tries to take two steps at a time, and down we go.

No matter how mature a Christian may be, no matter how

keen his knowledge of the truth or the depth of his experience with God, he is still prone to hesitate, blunder, fall into mistakes, errors, sins, even to the end of the road. But like other babies, Abram was picked up and he learned to walk more steadily.

Verse 3: Hagar . . . the Egyptian

The devil is always present in a temptation. We know from James (1:13) that God never tempts a man to sin. The evil in temptation comes from the enemy. The fact that Sarai had brought an Egyptian maid from Pharaoh's court shows the danger of sojourning in the world. When one leaves the world, something of it comes with him, and it must ultimately be disavowed and cast out.

It is highly significant that Hagar was an Egyptian, for that means she was a child of Ham, upon whom God pronounced the curse through Noah. Here Satan is seeking to put a counterfeit heir in the place of the promise. The consequences of any sin flare out as a chain reaction.

After . . . ten years in the land

After years of desert walk from Ur to Canaan, and now ten years in the land, yet Abram was just as prone to sin as before.

We sometimes sing, "Each victory will help you some other to win." In a limited sense, that is true, but in a vital sense it is not only not true but is exceedingly false. Trusting in victory ends in defeat. If we take our eyes from Christ, we will fail miserably. " . . . let any one who thinks that he stands take heed lest he fall" (I Corinthians 10:12, RSV).

Three things combined to lead Abram away from the promise: (1) Sarai was barren; (2) Hagar was at hand; and (3) Sarah urged him on. Abram was a man with earth's passions. It would take more than ten years in the land to stop him.

Verse 4: She conceived

Abram was so excited by the wonder of the promise of fruitfulness that he was willing to try carnal means to realize it.

Those who are truly zealous for God frequently reach for fruit without first dying. Unfortunately much Christian work is done in this way, and while there is conception, the child that is born can never be the heir. Christian work that is done merely through the zeal of human effort without counting the body as

124

dead, and Sarai as good as dead, may produce great revival campaigns with but a few genuinely saved, large church memberships with many tares among the wheat. God must condemn the issue of the union of the law with faith.

Her mistress was despised in her eyes

We are told that "Pride goes before destruction" (Proverbs 16:18, RSV). In a community of tents, nothing could be done in secret, and all Abram's world knew that he had gone in to Hagar. As soon as she knew that she was with child, her spirits rose within her, and she despised her mistress. Hagar realized that she was a woman fulfilling the functions of womanhood while Sarai remained barren. This reaction was quite natural, for human nature is like that. Sarai should have foreseen this. And so should we realize that the results of sin are inevitable. The fruit of the wind is the whirlwind.

Verse 5: My wrong be upon thee

The first result of the sin was pride, the second was jealousy that turned Sarai into a harridan. Sarai represents grace, and she had expected to be "built up" by Hagar, the law. But all she got was the humiliation that came from exalting a bondslave. Unreasonably, she turned against Abram. Her words may be interpreted, "My wrong belongs to thee as well," or, "May the wrong that has come to me be put on thine account."

It is the first reaction of the flesh to put the blame elsewhere, at least partly. Adam placed the blame back on God; Eve placed it on the serpent; Sarah seeks to place it on Abram. God places it upon our own old nature (Mark 7:20-23).

Verse 6: Do to her as it pleaseth thee

Abram was in a spot, for Hagar belonged to Sarai. All he could do was to return her to the place of slavery. For Hagar represents the law, and the law cannot be cast out until faith has brought life out of death. Till then the law must be the handmaid of the Gospel, to slay us that God may make us alive. Only then may the law be cast out.

But how sad that it pleased Sarai to treat Hagar harshly! The poor bondslave could not have avoided the liaison with Abram. Wounded pride causes jealousy; the fruit of jealousy is cruelty. Thus does one sin bring another with it.

125

She fled

When circumstances are very hard, we try to run away, but how fortunate if our wayward steps lead us to a meeting with the Lord. Poor Hagar was an Egyptian and had no place in the covenant that God had made with Abram. Daughter of Ham, she was under the curse.

But her slavery and humiliation were leading her to the grace of God. Now that she was with child by Abram, she was to come under the special grace of God which He gives as He wills. The roughest pathway often leads to a mountain top where a magnificent panorama of grace lies before us.

Verse 7: The angel of the Lord

A study of this phrase with a complete concordance will reveal that this messenger of Jehovah was none other than the Lord Jesus Christ. It should be understood that an "angel" is a messenger and that God uses various orders of created beings — men, spirit beings, cherubs, seraphs, Satan, etc. — as "angels" as well as the Holy Spirit and the Lord Jesus Christ.

What a lesson in humility that the second person of the Godhead, "who thought it not a thing to be grasped at to be equal with God" (Philippians 2:6, RSV), was willing to be the messenger of Jehovah, and to come to a mistreated Egyptian slave girl! His mission was to bring her a blessing from the God of sovereign grace.

Found her

The God who sought Adam when he had sinned and ran to hide now finds Hagar who is in trouble. We may be sure that God is more interested in us than we are in ourselves. We see here that God never fails to see what is going on and that He is vitally interested in everything that touches one of His creatures. We may attempt to run away from the things that happen to us, but two things we can never get away from: we cannot elude ourselves, and we cannot get beyond God. As David put it, "If I take the wings of the morning, and dwell in the uttermost parts of the sea; Even there shall thy hand lead me, and thy right hand shall hold me" (Psalm 139:9, 10).

By a fountain of water in the wilderness

In many places in Scripture we find that water is a symbol

126

of the Word of God (cf. Ephesians 5:26), or of the Spirit of God (cf. John 7:38, 39). Here in the midst of the wilderness which is the world, God has a fountain of water for His own.

When we run away from our circumstances, we shall be found by God when we stop by the fountain of the Word. A student came to see me in trouble, and I spoke to him of his Bible. It was in the bottom of the trunk, where he had put it when he left home four years before. He was out in the wilderness, but the fountain was in his trunk. There the messenger of the Lord had to find him.

Verse 8: Whence? . . . Whither? . . .

The questions of God are always for a purpose. He must bring us to ourselves. The Lord Jesus told that other woman at the well to call her husband, although He knew that she had none (John 4). It was in reality, "Whence comest thou? and whither wilt thou go?" and it brought the Samaritan woman to herself. Then she could be brought to the truth. The heavenly messenger brought Hagar to herself; and from thence she was brought to the place of blessing.

Verse 9: Return . . . submit . . .

If we seek to change our circumstances, we will jump from the frying pan into the fire. We must be triumphant exactly where we are. It is not a change of climate we need, but a change of heart. The flesh wants to run away, But God wants to demonstrate His power exactly where we have known our greatest chagrin. Life's disappointments are frequently His appointments.

When we come to the end of ourselves, we can begin with God. It may be humiliating to be forced to return to the place of failure, but that is where His power will enable us to triumph. Neither God nor the schoolteacher forces you to take a year over again if you have passed the examinations. Only when we have failed, must we go back to the beginning.

Verse 10: I will multiply thy seed

Not for an instant does God acknowledge the union of Abram and Hagar as a real marriage. He sends Hagar back, not as a wife to Abram but as a servant to Sarai. But He sends her back with a great promise. Her seed will be multiplied exceedingly. The promise accompanies the demand.

When He says, "Return . . . submit . . . ," His blessings always accompany such return and submission. This promise is to encourage us when the flesh would certainly shrink from doing the hard thing. The mother returns readily to bondage when she realizes that it will be blessing for the child. The Christian walks readily in the way of the Lord when he knows it is for his eternal fruitage.

Verse 11: Ishmael

Since God is Lord over all, He can enter into our lives in His providence and we can surely be blessed. Hagar was so blessed; she was to have a child whose name was dictated by the Lord. Throughout her life this name would ring in her ears to remind her of the faithfulness of God. For Ishmael means "God shall hear." The name would sound in her ear like the clapper of a bell. The melody of God's love and provision for her and the child, and of her love for him and for the Lord would make the full harmony within her soul. Thus when we feel abandoned and alone, while our need grows day by day in the womb of life, we may know that our God is our refuge.

The Lord hath heard thy affliction

Nothing can ever touch the object of God's love without passing through that love. Anything that has been sifted through the love of God has lost all power to hurt us. Many verses show that God is especially attentive to the cry of those who are in distress. Nothing can touch us that does not touch Him. Of His people it is written, "In all their affliction He was afflicted" (Isaiah 63:9). One of the most comforting thoughts in the revelation of God is that we are loved by God even more than we love ourselves.

Verse 12: A wild man

Literally a "wild-ass man." That is, he was to be a free nomad. We believe that here is the first indication of the far-reaching effects of the sin of Abram. It should not be forgotten that Ishmael is the father of the nomadic peoples of the desert, and that today, the Arabs, as followers of Mohammed, are the great opponents of Israel, standing across the land and barring the way of the rightful seed to possession of the inheritance which is theirs by promise. The father of the faithful had begotten a wild-ass man instead of a child of grace. This is God's judgment on the fruit of self-effort.

Verse 13: She called the name

This tremendous revelation is given to an Egyptian slave girl. She realizes Jehovah Himself is speaking to her. She is the first woman at the well, and to her as to the Samaritan, He says, "I who speak to you am he" (John 4:26).

Such a revelation of the presence of the living Redeemer outweighs all the sorrow or trial that comes in life before He is known. It is not only true for the afterlife of heaven that the sufferings of this present time are not worthy to be compared with the glory that shall be revealed in us (Romans 8:18). The believer can say that the sufferings of the present time are not worthy to be compared with the glory which He gives to us the moment we are aware of His presence.

Thou God seest me

This verse is like a coin with head and tail. We have looked at the reverse in the previous paragraph, but let us see its meaning as it burst from the heart of this poor woman, great with child, who had fled from Sarai's jealousy and cruelty.

Hagar learned that all which happened to her was known to the heavenly Father who was interested in her sighs, and groans and cries. She had seen that God was able to meet her in the midst of her need and to extricate her from all her difficulties. In the midst of trouble, we are tempted to think that our case is desperate, but at the fountain in the wilderness He teaches us that He looks upon all our afflictions.

Have I here looked after him

The meaning is obscured in most translations. The word "after" does not refer to the direction of her look, but to a time sequence. We might translate it, "Did I ever look at anything else after He gazed upon me?" When God truly reveals Himself to the soul, the sight can never be lost. It is the sight of His love that arouses love in us, and we love Him because He first loved us (I John 4:19).

Verse 14: The well . . . Beerlahairoi

The meaning of the name is: "The well of the Living One who seeth me." We are told in the New Testament that "it is a fearful thing to fall into the hands of the living God" (Hebrews 10:31). But we can say with positive assurance that it is a wonderful thing to be found in the heart of the living God.

To know that God is not an idol . . . How wonderful! To know that God is more than an impersonal force . . . To seize the fact that we are not dealing with a distant deity who must be approached through priests or other intermediaries . . . Here is the characteristic of the true believer . . . His God lives and reigns. When we know that our God is alive, our wells will be named for Him, and we will draw all our waters there.

Verse 15: Abram called his son's name . . . Ishmael

Where did Abram get that name? When Hagar returned to the camp, she bore such a testimony that she convinced the old man that the God who had revealed Himself to him in Ur had now been pleased to reveal Himself to this servant maid. One who has truly seen the living God will have a witness that sweeps all before it. There is no controverting the man who has been to Calvary and has come away alive forevermore.

Hagar accepted the hard command to return and submit. She went back refreshed with a water that did not come from the well by which she had wept. She convinced Abram and he named the baby as God had told her to name him.

Genesis 17

Verse 1: Ninety years old and nine

It is never too late for God. There is no such thing as age for the One who is Himself the eternal One, the alpha and the omega, the beginning and the end. One who is truly a child of God will be carried by Him to the end. The good work begun in us is to be performed, not till we are old and feeble, not until we die, but until the day of Jesus Christ (Philippians 1:6). God is concerned not with the outward man that perishes, but with the inward man, so that he may be renewed day by day (II Corinthians 4:16).

The Lord appeared to Abram

Again and again this happened. God is teaching us — since He tells us that these things were written for us (Romans 4:23, 24) — that He will come to us with fresh supplies of grace for every step in our development and growth with Himself. Nothing can cause the soul to grow except the knowledge of our God, obtained in this age, through His Word.

This is not the day of visions and divine appearances, any more than Abram's day was a day of the written Bible. What God did directly for Abram, was done sporadically. How vastly, yes, infinitely, greater is our advantage in possessing the Holy Spirit who dwells within us, and teaches us through the objective Word which He has given us.

Almighty God

Abram's new need brought a fresh revelation of God and a new name of God to delight his soul and open new vistas on the wonder and being of the God of glory who first appeared to him in Ur. Our English word comes from the Greek which translates the Hebrew in other passages, and includes the idea of "might," but this thought is not in the Hebrew.

The dictionaries say the meaning is unknown, but the Hebrew is *El Shaddai,* and there is a common noun *shad* which means "breast," and I believe that the spirit or theology of the passage demands that the meaning be found in the name. God, then, is the One on whose breast His children find their rest and from whom they would draw their nourishment.

Walk before me, and be thou perfect

God never demands anything that He has not already provided. The believer has merely to draw on the resources that have been made available. Revealing this name of God was like Moses' striking the rock — the stream gushed forth and Abram was refreshed. He now understands, more clearly than before, the God with whom he has to do. Thus it is logical for God to command his walk and his growth. He is to walk before God and to be "blameless." The Hebrew word used here is elsewhere translated, "without blemish, complete, full, sincerely sound, without spot, undefiled, upright, and whole." God is saying: "I have opened an account, now draw on it."

Verse 2: I will make my covenant

All blessings begin with God, the One who blesses, and all promises come from Him. Man has nothing to give, but he satisfies the heart of God through the love that is returned to Him. Here is the guarantee of our salvation and the sureness of His covenant. What He has promised, He is able also to perform; and when He sets Himself to accomplish something, it is as good as done. For His covenant is an everlasting covenant (Hebrews 13:20).

I will multiply exceedingly

God never does anything by halves. His blessings carry an adverb "exceedingly." When infinity pours blessing into our pint cup, there is always an overflow. Our God even increases our capacity to hold more, and will continue to increase it forever.

Note that in Genesis 16:10 God promises to multiply Abram's

descendants exceedingly and now Abram himself is to be multiplied exceedingly.

Whenever God uses an individual, He not only blesses the work, He also blesses the worker. In fact, the worker is much more important to God. Work is getting work done. He could have the work done by angels, but He begets sons and then undertakes to enlarge them exceedingly.

Verse 3: Abram fell on his face

The realization of a great promise will always put us on our face before God who is seeking true worshipers to worship Him in Spirit and in truth (John 4:23). We may be sure that God is going to get what He is seeking, and we may glory in the fact that He has chosen us so that we might be to the praise of the glory of His grace (Ephesians 1:6). It is a chain reaction: God saves us, we thank Him, this thanksgiving pleases Him, He blesses us more, we bow before Him, He blesses us exceedingly, we fall on our faces, He changes our name by changing our nature, and the whole blessed process will continue forever and ever. He is the great giver, and He will give the most to those who will learn to be great takers.

God talked with him

How great is the condescension of God! The Creator of the universe forms man from the dust of the ground, puts life in him with His own breath, redeems him by love, and then makes him a companion and friend by filling the individual with Himself. This is indeed grace — marvelous grace.

Whenever God talks with a man in blessing, that man has been redeemed, justified, and set apart for God, and the things that God will say to the man are for his growth. We are to listen, and as soon as the conditions are fulfilled, He will pour Himself out in blessing to us. He even tells those who have ears to use them.

Verse 5: Neither . . . any more . . . Abram but . . . Abraham

In Hebrew God added one letter to Abram's name, the letter formed by breathing. In Hebrew, the name Jehovah is formed by the five vowels, I, E, O, U, A, with a twice-repeated H. The word for spirit, which means "breath," is *ruach* in Hebrew, which is pronounced by expelling air. God was adding His name to that of Abram.

Suddenly, as breath in the body of Adam brought life to the clay, so breath in the nature of Abram brought fruitfulness to this man of ninety-nine. It was the breath of God which Jesus breathed on the disciples in the upper room on the day of the resurrection (John 20:22). This Spirit of God will bring fruitfulness to us.

Have I made thee

Not a bit of this was yet fulfilled, but God puts it in the past tense because He is God. Abraham was a "máde man." He had come to the end of himself. At the age of ninety-nine he had reach *El Shaddai,* the source of all power. These are the two prerequisites to fruitfulness. So God pronounces Abraham fruitful. Now there is promise not merely of Isaac, but of many nations. We have not seen the end of this promise yet for the seed of Abraham is coming to its greatest day. It should be noted that God's promises are at first dimly seen, then they begin to unfold, as seen in the book of Genesis, and their greatness goes on forever: "A great nation" (12:2); "as the dust of the earth" (13:16); "as the stars" (15:5); "many nations" (17:5).

Verse 6: I will make thee exceedingly fruitful

After God says, "I have made you" (v. 5), He says "I will make you." That is always God's way. Promise precedes performance; and when we lay hold on the promise, we lay hold upon God. This method teaches us to look away from things and to fix our eyes upon the living God.

When I first studied this passage, I found seven promises in one paragraph, each beginning with *I will.* This set me searching the life of Abraham, and I found that there are three times seven promises beginning with *I will.* This is the secret of the life of Abraham — he was attached to the eternal source of all blessing and power. God wants to teach us that power and life do not come from ourselves but from His great *I will.* Abraham is to be "exceedingly fruitful."

Verse 7: I will establish my covenant

God's revelation of the covenant to Abraham is a slow process. The covenant had been made long ago, and if Abraham had

134

been impatient, he might have been inclined to doubt. But to the father of the faithful, the promise was as good as the fulfillment. He had learned the great lesson of resting quietly in God while God takes His time to do things in His own way.

Only people who are in the high gear of their own thoughts and ways are tempted to run ahead of God and do things in their own fashion. Later, they have to watch while their doings are undone and then they begin with God in His own time to do things in His way. What He has promised, He will establish.

Thy seed

The casual reader would think that the promise was made by God to Abraham and his children. But the Holy Spirit, the only true commentator of the Scriptures, explains in the New Testament that the Lord Jesus Christ was in view in this verse. We read, "Now the promises were made to Abraham and to his offspring. It does not say, 'And to offsprings,' referring to many; but, referring to one, 'And to your offspring,' which is Christ" (Galatians 3:16, RSV). We must be thankful that God did not make the promise to Abraham and his family only. We would have every reason to believe that their faithlessness had long since nullified the promises and destroyed all hope. But because God promised Christ, the promise must be fulfilled.

Be a God unto thee

This is the sum and substance of the covenant, and it contains all else, for if we have God, we have all else besides. In Him we live, and move, and have our being (Acts 17:28). Power belongs to Him (Psalm 62:11), and is given to us in Christ (Acts 1:8). Mercy belongs to Him (Psalm 62:12), and has flowed to us from Calvary. It is important to note that no strings were attached to this covenant. It was a flat — I will be thy God.

If someone had objected that Abraham would soon get out of the will of God again, the Lord would have answered — I will be Abraham's God. The covenant did not rest on the character or life of Abraham but on the nature of God. He was out after souls, and they were going to belong to Him by this covenant of mercy and grace.

And to thy seed after thee

One of the most wonderful thoughts in the Word of God is that He has promised to be faithful to believers and to save their children also. Salvation for the Philippian jailer included his household (Acts 16:31). Even where only one parent was saved out of paganism that one could claim the promises for the children of the marriage (I Corinthians 7:14). John said, "No greater joy can I have than this, to hear that my children follow the truth" (III John 4, RSV). Although this is true for a preacher and his spiritual children, it is even more true for the saved father and mother. To see one's own flesh and blood bowing at the feet of the Saviour passes every joy that earth can bring. We should pray for their *early* salvation, so that their lives as well as their souls will be saved.

Verse 8: I will give . . . I will be . . .

The Lord promised to give the land to Abram and his descendants, and He promised to be the God of Abraham and his descendants. The first was tangible; the second intangible. In later centuries, the children of Israel turned away from the invisible God and so lost the visible land. The time will come when the Lord will bring them back into the land, and they shall look on Him. Then Israel will truly possess the land.

When what God gives is more to us than the Giver, we may neither have the Giver nor the gift. But when the Giver is more than the gift, we shall have Him and with Him all the gifts. "But seek first his kingdom and his righteousness, and all these things shall be yours as well" (Matthew 6:33, RSV).

Verse 9: Thou shalt keep

Grace calls for faithfulness. An obligation goes with the nobility of our calling. The old knights said *Noblesse oblige,* and forced themselves to live up to the code of honor. The love of Christ must constrain us to live unto Him who died for us (II Corinthians 5:14).

When we learn that there is no power in us to fulfill our side of the covenant, we will also learn that God does not break the covenant because of our unfaithfulness. This will drive us back upon Him as never before, and grace will call forth new desires to be faithful. Ultimately, we learn that by coming to Him for fresh supplies of His grace, we grow in grace, and little by little we progress toward the fulfillment of our side of the covenant.

Verse 10: Circumcised

This is the first use of this word in the Bible, and it will appear often. The word as we have it, is Latin. *Circum* means "around," and we know it in such words as "circumnavigate" and "circumference." The other half of the word means "to cut." The act as God set it before Abraham, was to be a mark upon the bodies of all His people, as a sign that they were to cut away all things in their life which might hinder them from being fruitful.

A whole chapter is written in Romans (chapter 4) to show that salvation came to Abraham years before he was circumcised, so that this rite certainly had no saving merit. There we read that this was "a seal of the righteousness which he had by faith while he was still uncircumcised" (Romans 4:11).

Verse 11: A token of the covenant

God wants His people to be marked off from the world, and the mark must show in their flesh. Just as the Passover was replaced by the Lord's Supper, so the rite of circumcision was replaced by baptism, as definitely stated in the New Testament: "In him also you were circumcised with a circumcision made without hands, by putting off the body of flesh in the circumcision of Christ; and you were buried with him in baptism, in which you were also raised with him through faith in the working of God, who raised him from the dead" (Colossians 2:11, 12). It is evident, therefore, that baptism cannot save any more than circumcision did, since it is only a token of a covenant.

Verse 12: Eight days old

Our children are our most important possession; they must be marked from the Lord and for the Lord from their earliest days. The covenant was made by God with Abraham and with his descendants. This guaranteed that God would fulfill His promises to them; but, as we are taught in the New Testament, the blessings of the covenant were to be not only theirs who cut the flesh, but to them who "also follow the example of the faith which our father Abraham had before he was circumcised" (Romans 4:12, RSV).

When a parent presents his child to God, he is obligated to train the child in the way he should go; the presentation does not save the child; the child must walk in the steps of the faith of the parents.

Stranger

The obligation of faith was not only for the children born of Abraham, but for everyone under his control, even to the slaves who were bought with money from any foreigner.

Here, at the outset, we see the missionary nature of the faith that is ours in Christ. There was no promise to them directly, but if we can bring them in, buying them with the blood, the toil, the sweat and the tears of our love for souls and our missionary zeal, they, too, shall be included in the promise and will be marked off for God. Before the time of Christ, the only way whereby a Gentile soul might be saved was by adoption into one of the tribes, through circumcision, and then through the blood of the altar. Today the only way is through the cross of Christ.

Verse 13: My covenant shall be in your flesh

God had called Abraham, revealed Himself to him again and again, had given him the sevenfold promise, changed his name, putting His Spirit within him, but yet there remained a work to be done. Abraham must testify that there is nothing in the flesh of value, and he must take the knife to it in sign of the acknowledgment of the covenant.

Thus, says Paul, ". . . we are the true circumcision, who worship God in spirit, and glory in Christ Jesus, and put no confidence in the flesh" (Philippians 3:3, RSV). We are circumcised "by putting off the body of . . . flesh" (Colossians 2:11); "by the Spirit we put to death the deeds of the body" (Romans 8:13, RSV), and thus we bear in our bodies the marks of the Lord Jesus (Galatians 6:17).

Verse 14: The uncircumcised man child . . . shall be cut off

Let there be no false hope about entering into the glory of God apart from the way of death which He has established, and life through death. The first time Christ's blood was shed was at His circumcision; and shall not those who follow Him know

138

the knife in the flesh? We may not choose all the nice promises in which God makes provision to do everything for us.

The Word of God calls upon us to mortify the deeds of the flesh and to resist unto blood in striving against sin. We must see our God as a consuming fire and allow ourselves to be given up to death (II Corinthians 4:11). Certainly, the unsaved will be cut off from salvation, and the unsurrendered will be cut off from all reward.

Verse 15: Sarah

There was to be the breath of God in Sarah also, and thus a letter is added to her name as it had been to her husband's. She is almost ninety, but life begins at ninety for those in whom the breath of God is breathed. Heretofore, her name had been Sarai, "nobility," but now it was to be Sarah, "high princess." Thus does the Holy Spirit elevate those who put their trust in the Lord.

Verse 16: I will give thee a son of her

This was to be the son of the freewoman; this was the child of grace (Galatians 4:23). Isaac is the example of true fruitfulness.

If we long to bear fruit for the Lord in our lives, we must follow all the steps that have brought Abraham to this point. We must learn to know God in His glory, power and provision. We must trust Him as our shield and reward and as the source of all supply. He must breathe His Spirit into us, changing our name and our nature. Then the knife must be applied to our flesh so that we die to self, and mortify the deeds of the body. Only then shall we bring forth fruit unto God.

Verse 17: Then Abraham fell upon his face

Physical attitude in prayer and worship is not fixed by Scripture. Throughout the Bible, prayer was offered while standing, sitting, kneeling, lying in bed, and in other postures — eyes closed, eyes opened. The true believer will doubtless experience contact with God in all these postures. But unhappy the believer who has not fallen on his face before God.

Abraham . . . laughed

Abraham's mind was in a whirlwind. He was believing,

doubting, hoping, fearing, laughing all at once. His laughter was not the laughter of scorn, or was it of comic relief. Abraham was not laughing in joy or merriment. The context shows that it was laughter of astonishment which sometimes bursts from us involuntarily when we hear something that seems incredible and our mind races around the edges of it, seeking to comprehend it.

The Lord God is very patient with His children. He is like a parent teaching a baby to walk. He is so delighted by any attempt to take a step that He does not chide when the baby totters and falls. He rejoices in our growth and seeks to help us.

Said in his heart

The old man's body was prostrate on the ground in worship, his face was wrinkled in involuntary laughter, and his heart was expressing doubt. Soon he would ask God to do something alien to the divine will.

In his growing stages, a Christian can be very confused, but the Lord is going to keep right on with him in tenderness and patience, bringing him out of confusion and causing faith to emerge from doubt and confidence to come out of despair. This is God's process as He works to build in us that trust which will cause us to leap out of ourselves and rely wholly upon His Word, unsupported by outward evidence.

A hundred years . . . ninety years old?

Abraham was in the turmoil that follows an earthquake. A vast promise had hit him suddenly and he was shaken. Note that these words were spoken in his heart, not spoken aloud. He was adding up all the factors of unbelief. His own age plus Sarah's came to a total of one hundred ninety years of sterility.

The fourth chapter of Romans describes what was going on in his heart. The manuscripts differ in the rendition of verse nineteen. The King James Version says, "He considered not his own body," while the Revised Standard Version (and the Greek) says, "he considered his own body." Either way it means the same thing. He looked at the death within him and said, "It makes no difference," or he refused to allow that death to make a difference.

140

Verse 18: Abraham said unto God

Isn't it strange what nonsense we will sometimes say to God in our prayers: Remember that Abraham's body was prostrate in an attitude of worship and praise. Here we see the growth of faith. The promise is given. The body is thrown into an outward attitude of acceptance. The heart is churned with doubt. This turns to prayer, and the faithful old man asks God to do according to the human desire instead of according to the divine plan. The prayer is unintelligent. Even while pleading for his own will, the struggle ceases and doubt gives way to receptive faith.

O that Ishmael might live before Thee

This shows how much the human heart is addicted to desiring its own fruitfulness, and how foolish we can be even in the midst of our prayers. Ishmael had shown that tented world that Abraham was indeed a man, capable of begetting a child, so Ishmael had been the bulwark of Abraham's pride. He clings to that fruit of his flesh even while learning that God cannot receive or bless that which is born of the bondwoman by the power of the flesh. While receiving the promise of great, divine things, he pleads for the blessing upon little, human things. A child of Adam wants something that smells of Adam rather than to have the divine fragrance of heaven.

Verse 19: God said [no]

God does not grant our foolish requests. We are such ignorant babies when we pray! A girl once asked me to pray that a certain man would propose to her. I knew him to be no good, and three years later she thanked God that her hope had not been granted. God does not give us all the pretty things we want, and which would be to our undoing.

A baby cries for a sharp knife when he sees the sun glint from its blade, but no mother in her right mind would give the knife to him. God is in His right mind, and will not give us all the cutting edges we pray for.

Thou shalt call his name Isaac

How strange if our children were named according to the weaknesses of our faith! Abraham laughed, and God called the child's name Laughter. God did not give this name to rebuke

141

Abraham and Sarah for laughing at His promise. God was pointing out that after a halting walk of doubting, there comes real faith — faith bears fruit, and fruitfulness brings the laughter of true joy.

And so the name of the child of promise speaks of the joy of the Lord which is our strength. And we can never know that joy until we have turned from the flesh to the Spirit and learned the power of God to bring life out of our death.

Verse 20: As for Ishmael, I have heard thee

The blessing of Ishmael has carried with it the most terrible results of the centuries. Out of Ishmael came two horrible things — both of them great hindrances to the people of God. For out of Ishmael came the Arab race, which today bars the advance of Israel, the rightful owner of the land which God swore should belong to Isaac and his descendants. And from Ishmael came Islam which is the strongest threat to the advance of Christianity the world has ever seen.

I have blessed him

Surely this verse shows that God's ways are not our ways. For years Ishmael and Isaac lay on two sides of an armed line which cut across Jerusalem. The covenant has been established with Isaac, but there is blessing for Ishmael also. It is hard to get Jew and Arab to see this, but one day Ishmael will have his place in the land under the rule of Isaac.

It is hard for us to see that the fruit of our own evil doings can be a part of all the things that work together for our good, yet it is so because our God has said it. God who makes the wrath of man to praise Him can make even the stupidity of His children work out for His glory and their good.

Verse 22: God went up from Abraham

How inestimable our advantage over Abraham! When we have talked with God and have listened to His voice in the Word, brought to our hearts by the Holy Spirit, He does not leave us.

We have so much that Abraham did not have. If we are honest with God, we shall find that either the Holy Spirit is within us in fullness of power and joy, or that He is grieved and waits for us to fall before Him and acknowledge our sin that we may be cleansed and restored to fellowship. Christ said to His disciples that the Holy Spirit was *with* them and that He would dwell *in* them (John 14:17). And we are the ones who benefit by that change of relationship.

Verse 23: The selfsame day

There is only one true way to obey and that is with alacrity. The command was a hard one for it meant a painful mortifying of the flesh, but there was no hesitation. God spoke and the only thing to do was to obey. A soldier knows that he cannot argue with his captain about an order. No matter what he thinks about it, there is but one thing to do: Salute, right about face, execute the order. If we are to know the joy and fruitfulness of the Christian life, we must obey.

Verse 24: Abraham was ninety years old and nine

Chronologically, he was ninety-nine; spiritually, he was twenty-nine. It was that many years since he had seen the God of glory in Ur of the Chaldees. He had come from spiritual babyhood through spiritual childhood, through many dangers, toils and woes. He was now at the end of himself, willing to let God teach him that there was no good in the works of the flesh, and that hope was alone in the promise of God.

May we learn to grow faster and not lose so many years of our lives by being so slow to learn the way of faith. The Lord is always ready to bring us on as rapidly as we will let Him, but He will never skip any steps of the process; they are all vital.

Genesis 18

Verse 1: And the Lord appeared unto him

For every crisis there is a fresh supply from God through a fresh revelation of Himself. No matter what the stage of Abraham's progress, there was still more to know and thus it will be forever.

Abraham was now to be brought to the final stage of separation from Lot. He must see his beloved nephew brought to the edge of doom, his family lost, his wife judged, and himself stripped bare of all possessions. For the harrowing experiences to come, God gives Himself afresh to Abraham.

Lot (19:1)

We are now going to combine verses from chapters 18 and 19 for the great lessons they teach in the contrasts, so numerous that they are certainly divinely designed for our instruction.

Abraham is the father of the faithful; Lot is the father of the worldly Christian. Both are declared to be justified (Romans 4:3; II Peter 2:7). Abraham is the Christian who walks by faith; Lot is the Christian who walks by sight. Abraham turned to God; Lot turned to circumstances. Both entertained messengers from heaven; both welcomed these heavenly messengers. How different the spiritual life and the carnal life are seen by the contrast.

In the plains of Mamre
To Sodom (19:1)

Mamre means fatness, and it was in Hebron, which means communion. Here the Lord met Abraham. Sodom is the arch-picture of the world in all its corruption. The Lord appeared to Abraham in communion and blessing and began to reveal Himself and His plans to this highly-favored servant. The Lord had to seek out Lot in the midst of his carnal surroundings and deliver him by force. Abraham had in slow steps been brought on by God to intimacy and divine friendship which were now to yield rich results; Lot had gone on by selfish and willful choice to the place he occupied in the God-denying world.

We are living in fatness, in full communion with God, separated from the world, or we are living out of full communion, and in the midst of the world.

He sat in the tent door

Abraham was a pilgrim and a stranger. He never bought any land until he purchased a burying cave for Sarah's body. He looked for a city that has foundations, whose builder and maker is God (Hebrews 11:10). The more Abraham knew God, the less he was interested in the world and its things. Little by little, he was being separated from all things and he was being separated unto God. It is always true that separation *to* means separation *from*. Without doubt, the people who lived in the civilization of Sodom thought of the old man as an eccentric who looked down upon city comforts and was content to dwell in a tent. The worldly Christian can never see spiritual things that are visible to the eye of faith.

The gate (19:1)

In an ancient city, the gate was the place of honor. The industrious woman in the last chapter of Proverbs had a husband who was known in the gates, where he sat among the elders of the land (Proverbs 31:23). Lot had first pitched his tent toward Sodom (13:12), moved into the city (14:12), and then became a leader in the city.

Alas, the Christians who live in the world have never yet succeeded in reforming it, and never will. They themselves even lose their reward and are saved so as by fire (I Corinthians 3:15), God's purpose is not to cleanse or improve this world but to judge it, and to call a few Abrahams to the place where they will witness against it, while living for another world.

Heat of the day;
at even (19:1)

When the Lord comes to the growing believer who is separated from the world, who bears the marks of the dying of the Lord in his flesh, and who is testifying against the world that is arrayed against God, He comes as a heavenly guest in the full light of day, to bring His fellowship and true communion.

When the worldly Christian receives his heavenly visitors, it is in the fading light at evening. His day of life has been frittered away in useless pursuits in Sodom, attempting to correct the evils of a place instead of condemning them and leaving. One of the saddest sights of this world is a wasted Christian life.

Verse 2: Three men;
two angels (19:1)

To Abraham, this appearance was "God in three persons, blessed Trinity." In one sentence the men said something and in another moment Jehovah spoke. At times it says, "they said" and then "he said," and then "the Lord said." To Abraham was being fulfilled the promise, "If a man loves me, he will keep my word . . . we will come to him and make our home with him" (John 14:23, RSV). They came in a manner and form that Abraham could comprehend, and they lodged and ate with him in fellowship.

Lot received the heavenly messengers, only two. He did not know the power of the Holy Spirit. He knew God in creation and the Lord in redemption, but the Spirit is not known to the worldly Christian.

He ran to meet them;
he rose up to meet them (19:1)

The difference between the believer who walks by faith and the one who is walking in the world is evident by the manner in which each receives the Lord. Abraham, separated from the world, had no other Master but the Lord. There was nothing to preoccupy his attention, and when the Lord appeared, He ran to meet Him. The Holy Spirit upon Abraham drew him immediately to the Lord.

Lot was preoccupied with worldly things. He rose up to welcome the Lord, but there was no instinctive quickening of his

146

senses to be ready for the Lord and to welcome Him gladly. The carnal Christian must overcome the inertia of the world.

He bowed himself (19:1)

In both chapters, the outward attitude of worship appears to be the same, but the inner attitude of each man is different and will manifest itself in a dozen details. The whole being of Abraham was bowed to the Lord, his heart, soul, mind, strength, emotions, aims, ambitions, purposes, loves, desires and anything else that will express the inner man.

Lot bowed, but he was preoccupied. His mind was on the affairs of Sodom. His children would soon mock him; his townsmen would ridicule him, and his whole life would be seen as a raw, naked compromise.

Verse 4: Rest . . . ;
turn . . . (19:2)

Both Abraham and Lot sing "Abide with me . . ." but there is a great difference in the invitation and in its reception by the Lord. Abraham has long been yielded to the Lord, and so communion with Him comes quite naturally, and without any difficulties. He expects to give the Lord his best, and the Lord is easily entreated by him.

When a Christian confesses that his prayers are seemingly unheard, he is confessing that he is living the life of Lot. When a Christian has immediate and ready access to the Lord, we may be sure that it is because he has passed through the revelations of God's being and yielded to the mortification of the knife that has cut away the flesh.

Verse 5: So do;
nay (19:2)

Abraham had an immediate acceptance to his invitation. Lot is at first met by a rebuff. The Lord is easily entreated by those who are willing to die to the world and the flesh. Abraham had refused Sodom and had accepted the knife, so the Lord would fellowship with him. Lot had accepted Sodom and refused the knife, therefore the Lord says, "No."

These spiritual principles are as definitely laws of God as are the laws of gravity, and the laws that govern atoms. His good things are for those who walk uprightly (Psalm 84:11).

147

Verses 2, 6, 7: He ran; . . . hastened . . . ran

When a man who is about a hundred years old runs, you may be sure that something of great importance is at hand. Abraham ran to meet the guests; he hastened into the tent to tell Sarah; he ran to the herd to fetch a calf. The Lord was in his heart, and his heart went into his feet. God tells us that we are to do whatsoever we do "heartily, as serving the Lord and not men" (Colossians 3:23). Abraham may have thought that he was running to honor men, but God was his guest that day.

All will go swiftly if He is in the heart — the dishwashing, sewing, mending, office work, studying — in short, whatever we are doing. And even if the body is bedridden, the heart can run for God.

Verse 6: Into the tent

There was no hindrance to Abraham's reception of the heavenly guests. He went about the normal procedure of hospitality without wild alarms to disturb him. No worldly crowd, bent on lust, beat around his door as they did at Lot's. No raucous cries disturbed his communion with his guests. No struggle or compromise distracted him from waiting upon the Lord.

He was God's man in God's place, and so all went with the quietness and smoothness of the Lord's ways, all of which are ways of pleasantness, and all of whose paths are peace (Proverbs 3:17). His heart was not drawn aside by any other matters, for nothing stood between him and his service for the Lord.

Out at the door (19:6)

Lot's communion was disturbed and distracted. He was where he should not have been and the things of the world were bound to interfere. After the two messengers entered Lot's house, there is no record that he spoke to them. They did all the talking, and theirs were words of judgment and warning.

If we are carnal Christians, it cannot be otherwise. Abraham was able to talk with God and receive fresh promises of grace and new revelations of God's way and plans. Lot was busy with the world which he sought to improve, and he had no time to compose his thoughts for communion with his God. God may speak to us of judgment, but if we are to talk with Him, we must be where He wants us to be, then He will speak to us of blessing.

Verse 7: A calf;
a feast (19:3)

Abraham offered that which cost a blood sacrifice. The word for "feast" (which Lot made for the messengers) is translated "drink" four times in the first of Daniel, and is used in Esther ten times for the banquet of wine. Lot's service was acceptable, but Abraham's was more acceptable. It was composed of the two parts of the Levitical offerings: the blood offering for wine and the meal offering which was a sweet savor unto the Lord (Leviticus 2:2). Abraham may not have understood all that he was doing, but all that is written of him has been written for us (Romans 4:23, 24). The yielded soul can enter into the offering of all to the Lord.

Verse 8: Stood by them;
Lot . . . shut the door after him (19:6)

There is a vast difference in the communion between the Lord and a spiritual Christian and that between Him and a carnal Christian. Abraham had passed through various stages of spiritual growth, and the circumcision of his flesh had taken place. Lot had moved into Sodom and had become one of its leading citizens. When God comes to visit each, Abraham is in calm communion with the Lord, and while the heavenly guests eat with him, he stands by them in perfect peace.

Lot, on the contrary, has no word for the divine messengers, and when the world clamors at his door he has to leave the presence of the Lord, go out to the worldlings and shut the door behind him.

This is the ultimate price that must be paid by the man who thinks that he can do anything for the world which crucified Christ.

They did eat (19:3)

In both chapters we find that the Lord ate with His children. Both Abraham and Lot were saved. And God has said that if any man will open the door, He will come in and eat with him (Revelation 3:20). But in the same context, He said that He would rebuke and chasten those whom He loved (Revelation

3:19). Fellowship with Abraham was followed by the promise of a son and heir, and later God confided to him His divine plan. Fellowship with Lot was followed by stern judgment that ended in catastrophe for Lot's loved ones, and thus for himself.

Verse 9: Where is . . . thy wife?
take thy wife (19:15)

You never really know a man until you know his wife; there is a sharp contrast between Abraham and Lot. Yielded circumcised Abraham now had his wife where she should be. If God had asked this question when Abraham was in Egypt, he would have had to answer, "She is in Pharaoh's house" (12:15). But now she is in his tent where she belongs.

This is no declaration of inferiority, for wife and husband are one in Christ, and the man who does not know how to care for his wife will never get his prayers answered (I Peter 3:7). No man can ever be used by God in the highest way, if his wife is not one with him in spiritual things (I Timothy 3:5, 11). All Lot could do was to order his wife to flee, and she never fully escaped.

Verse 10: I will certainly return unto thee

God is never ahead of His time and He is never late. He works out all things after the counsel of His will. He had promised Abraham years before that he would have a child. The time was fixed, and God would bring to pass the full counsel of His will. It is the same with all the works of God. "Let patience have her perfect work" (James 1:4). One of faith's sorest trials is to wait for God's moment. God will not be pushed. "But when the time had fully come, God sent forth his Son" (Galatians 4:4, RSV).

Verse 12: Sarah laughed

Sarah had been occupied with deeds of hospitality, and the kindness with which this was rewarded by God called forth the latent evil in her heart and caused her to commit a sin, which brought upon her a rebuke.

My Lord

Human obligations are inferior to divine obligations, but even in the midst of her unbelief toward God, Sarah fulfilled her

150

obligation to her husband and spoke of him as her lord. The Holy Spirit picks this word out of the narrative and cites it in the New Testament as an example for all true believing women. So in the midst of great unbelief, God picks out the one little thread of faithfulness to divine principle and writes it down forever.

When God cursed the house of Jeroboam, He announced that dogs should eat the bodies of all except one. That one should at least have an honorable burial "because in him there is found something pleasing to the Lord" (I Kings 14:13, RSV). God never overlooks even a gesture.

Verse 13: The Lord said . . . wherefore

Doubt is unreasonable because faith is believing the Word of the only Being in the universe who cannot be mistaken. To fail to believe God is to disregard the entire history of His providence and His grace. God knows even the secret laughter of our hearts and some day He will demand an accounting. Because He is God, He must take notice of our unbelief and He must reprove it.

Sarah was looking at circumstances while faith must always look to God. God must demand of every member of His bride why we look on some other face than His. Surely we can trust the Man who died for us, and the heavenly Father who planned it all.

Verse 14: Is any thing too hard for the Lord?

Here God lays bare the fact that the groundwork of unbelief is a doubt of the power of God to perform what He has promised. God made water flow from a rock in the wilderness, yet the people doubted that He could furnish bread. Although He rained manna from heaven, they questioned whether He could furnish flesh.

Even Moses counted the soldiers and told God that there were not enough animals in the flocks and herds to feed them and asked, sarcastically, if all the fish of the sea would be secured for them (Numbers 11:22). God replied, "Is Jehovah's arm waxed short?" To Jeremiah, God said, "Behold, I am the Lord, the God of all flesh; is there anything too hard for me?" (Jeremiah 32:27).

151

Verse 15: Sarah denied

One sin starts a chain reaction. Sarah might have said that she laughed only as Abraham laughed when God told him that there was to be a child (17:17). This would not have been true, for Abraham's laughter undoubtedly had some of the joy of faith in it. But Sarah made a barefaced denial of her sin. Unbelief came first and a lie was its child.

The human heart is laid bare by God's question. The Adamic heart wishes to justify itself, to deny its sins or to conceal them. The flesh is unwilling to be brought into the light, for there it must be crucified with Christ, and it does not want the nails to tear it and death to end its control. But life can never come before death.

Nay, but thou didst laugh

God will not allow us to make Him a liar by denying our sin. His flat rebuke struck home so deeply that there was no need for any further reproof. And what grace is displayed here! He might have said, "Well, because you do not believe Me, it will not come to pass." But He is slow to anger and Sarah's unbelief did not make the Word of God of none effect.

In fact, none of His promises would be fulfilled were He to stop because of our unbelief. By the nature of His being, He must exercise the fullness of His grace. And though there is no mention of it in Genesis, we are told in Hebrews that "by faith Sarah herself received power to conceive" (Hebrews 11:11).

Verse 16: The men . . . looked toward Sodom

The wickedness of Sodom had gone up before the Lord. Now, with slow steps, judgment approaches the city. There is an atmosphere of great suspense in the narrative, for we know how wicked the city was. Why did God proceed so slowly? Why did He not blast out from heaven without stopping at Abraham's tent for a meal? All that comes to pass is for the edification of God's people. "Surely the Lord God does nothing, without revealing his secret to his servants the prophets" (Amos 3:3, RSV).

The Lord stands looking at this world today, and He tells His own of the judgment that is to come upon it. We stand before Him in the place of intercession, but He is looking at the world.

152

Abraham went with them

This is more than the mere gesture of hospitality. Little by little, we have seen Abraham separated from everything: first, his native country, his father's house, his father; then he was separated from the fat land of Palestine and from Lot. Next, he gave up the thought of riches, then the thought of blessing through Ishmael. Now he has to separate from Sarah, herself. For he is to enter into an intimacy with God where secrets will be communicated to him, so he must be alone with God.

The path of the true believer will be lonelier and lonelier, but it will always be more and more full of God who will more than make up for every human separation.

˙erse 17: Shall I hide from Abraham?

What amazing grace! The Lord of the universe and the God of creation stoops in condescension to confide His secrets to one of Adam's race. But there is a loneliness in the heart of God because His nature is love. He, the Almighty, seeks out Abraham, and not only calls him His friend, but reveals His˘ closest secrets to him.

Malachi tells us that God looks down upon the race and He is delighted when He finds some of His own who fear Him and think upon His name, that He keeps a book of remembrance in heaven to record every such thought as it comes to the mind of man. He looked down into the heart of Abraham and saw a man who was faithful to Him in the measure of his growth in grace, and to him God determined to reveal His secrets.

Verse 18: Seeing that Abraham shall surely become . . .

Certainly, God was not picking Abraham out because there was anything in Abraham. In grace God chose him alone (Isaiah 51:2) when he was nothing more than a hole of the pit. But in His own heart, God had love and mercy toward Abraham, and this had increased Abraham and made him great. Lifting Abraham so high made it possible for God to commune with him as friend with friend. Abraham had become great but his greatness was of God, and now God would honor him.

A king can lift a pauper to be a prince, and then he can visit him in the castle he has conferred upon him. This is God's relationship to Abraham.

153

All the nations of the earth shall be blessed in him

This is a definite prophecy concerning the Lord Jesus Christ. In the New Testament, we read, "And the scripture, foreseeing that God would justify the Gentiles by faith, preached the gospel beforehand to Abraham, saying, 'In thee shall all the nations be blessed'" (Galatians 3:8, RSV). Here is the clear announcement that the Lord Jesus would come from Abraham, that He would die for the redemption of believers who would come out of every nation.

Verse 19: He will command his children

Family discipline is very important and is constantly spoken of throughout the Word of God as a vital Christian virtue. A man is not to be an elder if he does not rule his own house well (I Timothy 3:4, 5). Eli forfeited the priesthood because of the sin of his children (I Samuel 3:13). God orders parents to train up their children in the way they should go, and states that the one who spares the rod really hates his son (Proverbs 13:24).

Abraham was not satisfied with giving good advice to his children; he commanded them. There was real authority in his household, and that authority was maintained for God. There is no greater human joy than to know that one's children walk in the truth (III John 4).

His household

Some people hate the doctrine, but the Bible does teach household salvation. In order to understand it, we must comprehend that salvation is entirely the work of God and that man's will has nothing to do with it (John 1:13; Romans 9:16). In the face of such flat statements we must know that even John 3:16 is given us as a litmus paper to test the baseness of the human heart. Left to himself, no man will put his trust in the Lord Jesus Christ.

Since salvation is entirely by the grace and sovereign will of God, why shall we not accept His promise that salvation is for our household (Acts 16:31), and that even where only one mate is a believer, one can appropriate the promises for the children (I Corinthians 7:14).

Justice and judgment

God desires righteousness to prevail among men and He is

154

vitally interested in all that goes on. There is no oppression that He does not see, and His ear is always open to the cry of the poor. Many passages reveal God's interest in the needy, the downtrodden, the widow, the orphan, and all who are oppressed. He hears the sighing of the prisoner, and no tears have been shed which have not been noticed by Him. His secrets will be revealed to those who are on the side of justice and judgment. To all those who draw their life from Him, and who seek to honor His name with righteous living, He will make Himself known.

The way of the Lord

Next to the Word of the Lord, the Way of the Lord is the most important thing in the universe. God has magnified His Word above His name (Psalm 138:2). A careful study of His ways will reveal all that He wants done, and all that He wants to do through us. The manner of doing is very important. For His ways are not our ways; in fact, He has told us that as the heavens are higher than the earth so are His ways above our ways (Isaiah 55:9).

In this particular verse, the way of the Lord is righteous living in justice and in judgment. The nature of the Lord is holiness, and He wants that holiness to be exercised among men. The day will come when we shall find that the Lord has noted every misuse of power and every deviation from His way of doing things, and that an accounting will be demanded.

Verse 20: The cry of Sodom and Gomorrah is great

Inanimate things have voices. Although we may not hear them with our ears, we must not be astonished that God can hear them. There are wave lengths of sound that are outside of the receptivity of our ears. Vacuum tubes catch these sounds and transpose them into bands which carry a sound to our ears. Someday man may even learn that stones and trees give forth sounds. At all events, the voice of Abel's blood cried to God (Genesis 4:10).

Here we find that the wickedness of two cities cried to heaven; unpaid wages cry to the ear of God (James 5:4). No injustice has ever gone unrecorded, there is no sin that has not shouted its presence to God. He who hears all will bring true righteousness in His time.

155

Verse 21: I will go down now, and see

God knew, of course, all that was taking place in the midst of Sodom. But now He is talking with Abraham, and condescends to speak like a human being. God is doing this to train Abraham in the walk of faith, and He is arousing in His child the spirit of intercession. During this present age, Christ is spending all of His time interceding for us (Hebrews 7:25).

Never are we more like Christ than when we are interceding. If we are to be true masters in prayer, there are two conditions — we must be well acquainted with the supply that is in God, and with the need of those for whom we pray. God comes down to us to reveal Himself and the world's needs.

Verse 22: Abraham stood yet before the Lord

The life of prayer is one of slow growth. Service may begin in running, even as ninety-nine-year-old Abraham ran at the first sign of hospitality's need (18:2, 6, 7). Communion with the Lord in the midst of service has brought further desire to prolong that sense of oneness, and Abraham has followed them all the way to the place where the road forked for Sodom. Two of the three went on, but one abode still with Abraham, and when one of the Godhead is present, all three are there. Something in the heart of Abraham arrested the Lord, who delights to be commanded by His children.

If we are going to know His will and His ways, we must go with Him, and yet stand before Him.

Verse 23: Abraham stood yet

We have God's promise that if we draw nigh to Him, He will draw nigh to us (James 4:8). In one sense, of course, He is always with us, even when our hearts are far from Him. But there is this blessed sense in which He is very specially with us when we draw nigh to Him. Abraham now comprehended that the men he had served, and who had given him the revelation of the coming birth of Isaac, were more than messengers, more even than divine messengers. He felt and knew the Lord Himself. To this his whole being responded and the Lord remained with him to reveal His ways.

The true growth of a soul is growth in the knowledge of the ways of God. There are many who know the Word, even more than superficially, who never know His ways.

Wilt thou also destroy the righteous?

The first error to be corrected in the mind of Abraham is that the death of righteousness means the destruction of the righteous. A little thought would have shown him that sudden death means sudden glory for those who are in Christ. Heavy bombing of a city means many souls enter into heaven.

In the case of the unsaved, the death of their bodies follows the death of their souls, and they are eternally separated, even as they are temporarily separated from Him while on earth. The righteous are in the world, but they are not of the world, and the judgment of the world can never touch them. All their judgment was borne by the Lord Jesus Christ.

Verse 24: Fifty righteous within the city

There is a solemn lesson here, for Abraham had casually overrated, fifty to one, the number of just persons in Sodom. How many born again people are in Philadelphia? London? San Francisco? Paris? Undoubtedly the proportion differs just as more people are saved out of a pagan tribe in black Africa than from a similar number of Moslems in North Africa. Abraham was thinking of outward appearances, but the Lord was looking upon the heart, and the true state of affairs was about to be uncovered by judgment.

It is a great picture of the last day, and makes us wonder if there are not many more tares in the midst of the wheat than we imagine. Thank God we do not have to decide who are lost and who are saved. That has been decided by the eye of omniscience and the heart of holiness and love.

Verse 25: Shall not the judge of all the earth do right

Abraham's supposed argument shows that he does not understand much of God and His ways. His talk is childish prattle. He has not learned that whatever God does is right, no matter how it may seem to the passing human who is incapable of forming a correct judgment. Only God can see the hearts of men and all the circumstances of life.

Many years passed before God revealed through the prophets that He was the potter and that He had power over the clay to do with it as He desired (Jeremiah 18; Romans 9:21). Instead of asking the Judge of the earth if He should not do right,

157

Abraham should have taken the position that whatever happened would be right because the judge of the earth did it.

Verse 26: I will spare all the place for their sakes

How much the wicked owe to the righteous! For their sakes blessings have been imparted to the undeserving and judgments averted from the wicked. For Jacob's sake God multiplied the flocks of Laban (Genesis 30:27); and out of respect to Joseph He prospered the house of Potiphar (Genesis 39:5).

If ten righteous could have been found in Sodom, the impending judgment could have been turned from all the cities of the plain; and notwithstanding the extreme wickedness of its inhabitants, the city of Zoar was exempted from the common fate, at the intercession of Lot; nor could the storm be poured upon Sodom, till Lot was placed beyond its reach (Genesis 19:22).

All in the ship were saved from death because Paul was there (Acts 27:24, 34), and God said He would spare Judah from the captivity if they could find one righteous man in Jerusalem (Jeremiah 5:1).

Verse 27: I . . . am but dust and ashes

Communion with the Lord not only increases our knowledge of what the Lord is in His wonder and power, but it increases our knowledge of what we are ourselves. Black cannot know itself if it is next to gray only, but when it is next to white, it can discern its own blackness. This has been the universal experience of God's people.

Jacob said, "I am not worthy of the least of all the steadfast love and all the faithfulness which thou hast shown to thy servant" (Genesis 32:10, RSV). Job abhorred himself in dust and ashes (Job 42:6). Isaiah saw himself as a man of unclean lips (Isaiah 6:5). Peter said, "Depart from me, for I am a sinful man, O Lord" (Luke 5:8). A man who does not know his own color hasn't been close enough to the Lord.

Verses 30-32: Thirty . . . twenty . . . ten

By this time Abraham's confidence in the number of righteous in Sodom was dwindling rapidly. The longer one remains in the presence of God, the more proper perspective he gains on the world and all that is therein.

Abraham was praying in the Holy Spirit, who burdens the believer only with those requests which God intends to grant. So Abraham was not led to intercede beyond the number ten. To one who comprehends the eternal nature of God's plan, "Prayer changes the one who prays," is more important than the thought of prayer changing things.

Let not the Lord be angry

As if the Lord would be angry at a child who is learning to walk! A mother watches her child pull himself to a standing position. She is thrilled. He tries to take two steps with the same foot and falls down. She does not spank him; she picks him up, kisses him and watches with joy as he learns to overcome the force of gravity. In her mind's eye, she visualizes the day when he will run a race and win it.

So it is with our God. He is the heavenly Father. He wants us to walk worthy of the calling wherewith we have been called (Ephesians 4:1, Colossians 2:6). He wants us to run (Hebrews 12:1). Therefore, we may be certain that He is never angry with us when we take our first steps.

Verse 33: Communing with Abraham

Abraham was God's friend. That man should need a friend is comprehensible; that God is in need of a friend is a stupendous revelation of His love.

Man needs a friend for counsel and advice. God needs neither. Man needs a friend for help in adversity; God is never in adversity. Man needs a friend for information when in ignorance; God knows all things. Why, then, would God need a friend? The answer is that God is love, and He wants to be loved. That is one thing He lacks and that alone we can give Him.

159

Genesis 19

Verse 2: Turn in . . . tarry all night

We have compared Lot with Abraham, we now look at him by himself. He was a righteous man (II Peter 2:7). He had the gift of hospitality which is one of the divine qualifications for being an elder in Christ's church (I Timothy 3:2). Indeed, Lot had such a high sense of the obligation of a host that he would have sacrificed his daughters to protect his guests. Of course it is never right to commit one sin to prevent another.

The Lord's messengers at first refused Lot's invitation, for even a good man, who has been living contrary to the will of the Lord, must not think that His favors are easily obtained. If Lot had been living in a tent in the hills, the Lord would have entered at once. It is possible for our hospitality to be in the wrong place.

Verse 3: He pressed upon them greatly

And so he should have, for he was about to entertain angels unawares (Hebrews 13:2). There are three positions in intercession, and Lot is in the middle position. Abraham prayed and received the Lord's presence immediately (18:5). Esau sold his birthright for a mess of pottage. "For you know that afterward, when he desired to inherit the blessing, he was rejected, for he found no chance to repent, though he sought it with tears" (Hebrews 12:17, RSV). Lot stands between these two men. He did wrong, but he urged them strongly, and the messengers came to him and ultimately delivered him.

160

They . . . entered his house

Lot truly belonged to God, though he had no business being in Sodom. Because God's messengers came inside, Lot was not only saved, he was "greatly distressed by the licentiousness of the wicked (for by what that righteous man saw and heard as he lived among them, he was vexed in his righteous soul day after day with their lawless deeds)" (II Peter 2:7, 8, RSV).

It may have been a pleasant house inside, but it was in a horrible neighborhood, and the neighbors were hell-deserving sinners who must be evicted from their city, their homes, their bodies, and from this world. Judgment was even then lodging in the house of their neighbor, Lot.

Verse 5: They called unto Lot

The consequences of Lot's compromise now become manifest. He had gone to Sodom and had taken up his abode among devilish people. He had not improved one citizen even one whit.

The principles of a believer are not the principles of this world which crucified Christ. The Christian who attempts to reform the world will find that the world wants none of it and none of him, unless he gives up his Christ and his principles, and compromises with them. "They are surprised that you do not now join them in the same wild profligacy and they abuse you" (I Peter 4:4). The only thing that can be done for an ungodly world is to pray for it, testify against it and announce the judgment that is to come.

Verse 9: This one fellow came in to sojourn

To understand this sentence, we must hear the tone of sneering contempt with which it is spoken. The world has no respect for a compromising Christian. You never see a headline identifying a criminal with any lodge, trade or organization, as though it were strange that one with such associations would have sinned. But even though the relationship were twenty years in the past, newspaper reporters will seek to identify someone caught in sin as a former choir singer or a former Sunday school teacher.

It is a public confession that the world expects Christians to be holy. Lot may have tried to justify his presence in Sodom to himself or to his neighbors. He may have convinced him-

self, but there was not a man in Sodom but knew that Lot
had no business to be there.

Verse 10: The men . . . shut the door

If someone would wonder why God's angels let Lot get into
such a situation in the first place, the answer is that God never
forces a soul. Every choice by a Christian is his own. He lets
at least some Christians go through every horror that a worldling
can know, and the believer trusts Him in the dark.

Verse 11: They wearied themselves to find the door

The heart of man is indeed "deceitful above all things and
incurably sick" (Jeremiah 17:9, Heb.). Nothing will turn the
unregenerate man from the cycle of his instinct to sin. Life in
prison does not cure criminals. Physical blindness did not cool
the mad lust of these men of Sodom.

Verse 12: Hast thou here any besides?

Lot will have nothing to show for all his years of social
service in Sodom. A dung heap cannot be perfumed. Politics
cannot be reformed. Appetites cannot be slaked. Prohibition
will not prohibit. No soul was ever won by stooping to its level.
Improving an environment never helped its inhabitants. Lot did
not abide in the Lord, and he was, therefore, cast forth as a
branch (John 15:6). Being a believer, he was not cast out, but
God gave him no fruit. He was saved, but so as by fire (I
Corinthians 3:15).

Shall I hide . . . that thing which I do? (18:17)
Verse 13: The Lord hath sent us to destroy it

How differently God addresses a spiritual Christian from
the way in which He speaks to a carnal Christian. Abraham
and Lot each received a revelation of the coming destruction of
Sodom. To Abraham, walking with God, the Lord quietly
revealed His secret. To Lot, walking with the world. the Lord
gave a stunning warning of judgment and dragged him from the
condemned place before destroying it.

Lot would not have been interested in a quiet communication
of truth such as that which God gave to Abraham. Lot loved
Sodom, even while he loved the Lord, so God could not speak

162

to him as to a spiritual man, but as to carnal man, even as to a babe in Christ (I Corinthians 3:1).

Verse 14: He seemed as one that mocked

The Bible everywhere forbids mixed marriages. If Lot had not gone to Sodom, his daughters would not have acquired Sodomite husbands. His unmarried daughters were saved out of Sodom, but the smell of the place was upon their lives ever afterward. "Do not be mismated with unbelievers" is a divine command, and there are solid reasons to back up the order. There can be no fellowship between the light of a Christian life and the darkness of an unbeliever's life (II Corinthians 6:14).

Nehemiah tells the terrible story of the children of Ashdod and Israel who spoke half in one language and half in the other (Nehemiah 13:24). Nehemiah cursed them and pulled their hair out. The marriages of Lot's daughters had produced similar confusion.

Verse 15: The angels hastened Lot

It is a sad commentary when Christians have to be pushed into the things which are for their own good. Here is the true meaning of the word which unfortunately has been rendered "backslider." The word is not in the New Testament and the idea conveyed by the English word "slide" is not in the Old.

The true meaning is here illustrated by Lot's conduct. He was holding back. "Israel holdeth back as a backholding heifer" (Hosea 4:16). Any stockman who has loaded a truck with heifers will understand. Sheep can be loaded with almost no difficulty, pigs with more noise but without much difficulty. Heifers are like backholding men. They must be pushed.

Verse 16: He lingered

How could Lot have any affection for a place where the inhabitants were so filthily depraved as to come to his door at night seeking to vent their depravity upon his guests? How could a just man linger in a city where he had almost been forced to sacrifice the honor of his daughters? It is an amazing picture of the lust of the flesh against the drawing of the Spirit. Any man who thinks that his fleshly appetites will be stilled while he is on earth has not comprehended the baseness of Lot's desires, nor, indeed, his own.

163

The Lord being merciful . . . they set him without the city

It may have seemed unkind at the moment, but it was the Lord's mercy. To be pushed and pulled by an angel may not be pleasant, but it may be very necessary. God knows that death must fall on certain spots, and He does not want us on those spots. "It is of the Lord's mercies that we are not consumed." And the reason for these mercies, and those in pushing Lot out of Sodom, is "because thy compassions fail not. They are new every morning; great is thy faithfulness" (Lamentations 3:22, 23). It was good for Lot that the Lord's compassions were new that morning.

Verse 17: Look not behind thee, neither stay thou in all the plain

Whether Lot lingered because of love of friends, grief at the thought of losing his property, because he thought there was yet time, or obstinate belief that Sodom was still capable of amendment, we do not know. The angels had to use drastic measures and dramatic language. The time of God's vengeance was at hand. There was no safety now except in precipitate flight. There was no refuge except that which God would appoint.

The message and the manner of its presentation are applicable today. The New Testament tells us that "Sodom and Gomorrah and the surrounding cities . . . serve as an example by undergoing a punishment of eternal fire" (Jude 7, RSV). Probably for this reason, eternal punishment is described in similar terms.

Escape to the mountain

Even in sight of Sodom, God had provided a mountain of refuge. Even in sight of where we are, God has provided the mountain of Calvary. If we have escaped to the Lord Jesus Christ, no judgment can fall upon us, no storm can beat upon us. Justice has been satisfied forever, and wrath has been eternally stilled. "The name of the Lord" is a strong tower; the righteous man runs into it and is safe" (Proverbs 18:10, RSV). Let not any man think himself saved, if he lingers in the place of impending judgment.

He who lies down in Sodom is not a born-again man. It makes no difference if he can see the mountain from where he is lying, or if he cries out that his only hope is in the mountain. He must flee to the mountain and take sides with God against Sodom.

Verse 18: And Lot said unto them, oh, not so, my Lord

It seems incredible that Lot should argue with his rescuers, but drowning men sometimes fight those who seek to keep their heads above water. Lot's prayer was in earnest, "Not Thy will but mine be done." He had been praying this from the first moment, years before, when he chose the lush pasture near Sodom. His petition is full of egotism. Although he piously talks about the grace and mercy of God in saving his life, he is still determined to have his own way. The flesh is enmity against God, and it lusts against the Spirit.

Dust and ashes (18:27)
Verse 19: Behold thy servant

The contrast is maintained to the end. Where Abraham prayed to the Lord, he took his proper place and saw himself as dust and ashes.

Lot, while fighting a rear-guard action at every step to get his own way, pleads that he is the Lord's servant. God commands him to escape to the hills and he replies, "I cannot escape to the hills." He discounts God's providence and speaks of some imaginary evil that may befall him. He mutters about the mercy of God in saving his life and then intimates that the rescue was in order to imperil the life that has just been saved. The tragedy is that there is more prayer of this type than of the prayer of Abraham. This, indeed, is the sin of presumption.

Verse 20: It is a little one

The little sin is most dangerous, for it always leads to greater sins. In Africa, a missionary told a native helper that there was a little snake hiding in the pile of stones. The African looked at it and drew back with great care, saying, "Oh, Teacher, that is not a little snake. That is a very big snake. It is bigger than the boa constrictor. The name of that snake is, 'You-won't-get-home.'" The natives know that if they are bitten by that snake, they will die before they can reach home. A boa has no poison, and even though he crushes a man's bones, the man might live; but the bite of the little snake injects poison into the blood.

Let me escape thither

The Lord had commanded that he go to the hills for safety; Lot still lingers in the plain. It is hard to understand why the believer wants his own way so much until we study the Word of God and learn what the old nature really is. There is nothing that a man will not do to get his own way.

Lot had left Sodom and its grosser sins, and was advancing to the place of refuge, yet his heart was attached to the things which he had renounced. Many Christians wish to substitute the world of Zoar for the world of Sodom. They will ask for anything rather than have the separation of the lonely mountain.

Is it not a little one?

God records the whimperings of Lot to show us what we are in ourselves, and how we will plead for our own way. But we must remember that the little foxes spoil the vines (Song of Solomon 2:15). Moses chose affliction with the people of God, and the reproach of Christ rather than the pleasures of sin for a season, and the treasures in Egypt (Hebrews 11:25, 26). The reason was that he realized that God would do more for him than he could do for himself. Lot had not learned this and begged for even the little city.

My soul shall live

Lot had everything upside down. His soul would not live; his soul would languish. He would lose everything that was worthwhile and come into an oblivion that prophesies the emptiness of those who enter the presence of God without any fruit.

Verse 21: I have accepted thee concerning this thing also

The terrible mystery of the grace of God is wonderful to contemplate. Was the sparing of Zoar the gracious answer of the mercy of God or the terrible judgment upon a justified man who refused to yield to the grace of God? Was God kind to Lot, or was he delivered over to his own desires? I incline toward the latter view. For I recall the story of a boy who stole sugar and who was forced to eat a half cup of the stuff for breakfast, lunch, and dinner until he sobbed out his promise not to steal any more.

God's ways are ways of pleasantness, and *all* His paths are peace (Proverbs 3:17); therefore the disastrous result of Lot's choice proves that it was not God's choice for him. It was God's permissive will, but not His directive will. God had directed Lot to the hills.

The which city thou hast spoken

God destroyed Sodom because there were not ten righteous people in it. God spared Zoar which had no righteous people, because a stubborn, carnal believer prayed for it for purely selfish reasons. It received at least a temporary lease on life because a believer chose to flee to its walls. Terrible is the heart of man, and wonderful is the grace of God by contrast.

Verse 22: I cannot do any thing till thou be come thither

What a startling example of the patience of God toward the wicked because of the presence of the saved among them! The world hates the believers and yet our Lord speaks of them as "the light of the world" (Matthew 5:14), and "the salt of the earth" (Matthew 5:13). Without the presence of the believers, the world would be shrouded in utter darkness, and the unsalted mass would speedily manifest its rottenness.

The only knowledge of God in the earth is that of His eternal power and Godhead (Romans 1:20) apart from that which shines through born-again ones who enlighten the darkness around them.

Verse 23: The sun was risen upon the earth

God never does anything in the darkness, because He is light, and in Him dwells no darkness at all. Sodom's sin was committed in the darkness, but God judged it in the darkness, and will even make manifest the counsels of the hearts (I Corinthians 4:5).

Verse 24: The Lord rained . . . fire from the Lord

Judgment has its source in God. Judgment is decided by God, executed by God. Do not think that the devil will punish any man. The terrible thing about the doctrine of eternal punishment is that God runs hell, and God will manage the lake of fire. The devil has never yet been punished, and when he reaches the place of torment, he will be the chief victim, not the jailer.

The fact that God is in three persons and yet is one God is

167

further seen here. The Lord was on earth, the Lord was in heaven, and all that They did is said to be done by Him. They are He and He is They. Herein is the certainty of judgment upon every abomination.

Upon Sodom and upon Gomorrah brimstone and fire

These cities are a mirror of life in our times. We are authorized by God to address the cities of our times by the names of these cities. "Hear the word of the Lord, ye rulers of Sodom and ye people of Gomorrah" (Isaiah 1:10). Though there are multitudes in our cities who abhor the depravity of Sodom, the causes of that wickedness are prevalent amongst us. "This was the guilt of your sister Sodom: . . . pride, surfeit of food, and prosperous ease" (Ezekiel 16:49, RSV). Certainly these cities never dreamed of luxury, and plenty and a love of ease equal to ours.

Verse 25: He overthrew those cities, and all the plain

What God did to these ancient communities He has promised to do to our land, to the whole world, and to all of the human race. The Lord Jesus said, "Likewise as it was in the days of Lot — they ate, they drank, they bought, they sold, they planted, they built, but on the day when Lot went out from Sodom fire and brimstone rained from heaven and destroyed them all — so will it be on the day when the Son of man is revealed" (Luke 17:28-30, RSV).

This is a description of our civilization. We are absorbed in all the affairs of business, social, political and even religious life.

Verse 26: Lot's wife looked back

Lot was advancing to a place of refuge; his wife was following, but her heart was truly in Sodom, even though Lot had renounced the city. To all such we should trumpet forth the words of the Lord Jesus Christ, "Remember Lot's wife" (Luke 17:32). Was it curiosity, or longing, or love for friends or neighbors? Her motives do not matter. The fact is that she looked back, and consequently she was instantly struck dead by God. For looking back, she became a monument to all future generations that God demands that we turn wholeheartedly away from Sodom.

A pillar of salt

If this is literal (and I believe it is), then we can see how terrible it is to be tares instead of wheat. Her heart in Sodom, the woman was only savorless salt, and her physical body was transformed in judgment as a monument to warn against carnal love and its association with the most depraved in judgment. The warning comes to us, "Do not love the world or the things in the world. If any one loves the world, love for the Father is not in him" (I John 2:15, RSV).

Verse 27: Abraham gat up early in the morning

It would appear that Abraham had gone home (18:33) and God had given him a good night's sleep. The old man was ninety-nine, but refreshed, he wakes in the morning to go back to the place where he had stood in sweet communion with the Lord and had cried to God in intercessory prayer. God is more eager to meet with us than we are to meet with Him. This is one of the mysteries of grace.

To the place where he stood before the Lord

Abraham had rested in the Lord and now he would return to the Lord. Israel was told through Isaiah, "In returning and rest you shall be saved; in quietness and in trust shall be your strength" (Isaiah 30:15, RSV). These things Abraham possessed because they possessed him.

We are always in the place of the Lord, for we stand on the blessed side of Christ's promise, " . . . the hour is coming when neither on this mountain nor in Jerusalem will you worship the Father" (John 4:21). God does not live in a building or in a reserved sacrament, but in the hearts of those who have been born again.

Verse 28: He [Abraham] looked toward Sodom

There is no record here of any word spoken by Abraham or that he ever saw Lot again. We may draw certain inferences from this silence. Certainly Abraham loved Lot, but now he has become completely separated from him. He had taken sides with God against his nephew. What he had been commanded to do forty years before when the God of glory appeared to him in Ur (Acts 7:2; Genesis 12:1), he had finally accomplished.

169

There is a terrible postscript about Lot, but there is no evidence that Abraham knew it.

There must be complete obedience to God, and a complete separation in our minds, even from our kindred, before we can be fruitful for God in His way.

The smoke of the country went up

We are not told one word about Abraham's reaction to the terrible scene that lay before his eyes. We can infer that he agreed with God and that the judgment had been fully earned by the cities, and they should take delivery of that which they had paid for.

Verse 29: God remembered Abraham, and sent Lot out

God did not spare Lot for Lot's sake but because of Abraham. When God destroyed the cities, He remembered Abraham. This principle is frequently illustrated in Scripture. When Israel made a calf of gold, God spared them not for their sakes, but because of Moses. In the prophets, we find that God looked for a man to stand in the gap (Ezekiel 22:30).

God is seeking to form Christ in the lives of His own, and no man is more like Christ than when he is interceding for the people of God, for this is Christ's entire ministry at present (Hebrews 7:25).

Verse 30: Lot went up . . . and dwelt in the mountains

One of the most dangerous things that a Christian can do is to move without the leading of the Holy Spirit. Lot had been running his own life. He pitched his tent toward Sodom (13:12), moved into the city (14:12); sat in the gate (19:1) and became a judge (19:9). When God pushed him out he pleaded for Zoar and moved into it. He knew immediately, of course, that the cities had been destroyed, even though he did not look back to see their destruction. And now, fretful, as any believer is when out of the will of God, he casts about for somewhere to go and for something to do. He remembers that the angel had told him to go to the hills, so he goes without permission or leading, and he meets spiritual disaster.

He feared to dwell in Zoar

When a man is out of the will of God, he is haunted by

bogeys of his own imagination. Lot refused to go to the hills when God told him to go for fear some evil would overtake him and he would die (verse 19). He thought he would be all right in Zoar, but fears rose again as he found himself in a small city in the midst of a burnt-out region.

This proves that Lot loved only himself and not God, for "There is no fear in love; but [His] perfect love casts out fear. For fear has to do with punishment, and he who fears is not perfected in love" (I John 4:18, RSV). No matter where he goes, he must take himself along, and thus his problem is ever with him.

In a cave

Abraham lived in a tent, and beside it he had an altar. Lot reached the hills of refuge but instead of the free communion with God, he chose to abide in the place of death, as throughout the Bible, the cave is frequently the symbol of the tomb. The only cave that Abraham owned was the one which he purchased to be the tomb of Sarah. Lot, like the woman who lived in pleasure (I Timothy 5:6), was dead while he lived. It was quite fitting that he chose the cave for his abode, and it was the scene of his final corruption and downfall.

And his two daughters with him

The sad loneliness of Lot may excite our pity, but we take sides with God against him, and we acknowledge that he was eating the fruit of his own doings. He had chosen Sodom, and had left there his reputation, his life's work, his friends, his wife, and his sons-in-law. God, in His covenant dealings with His people, was gracious enough to rescue his daughters, but they brought the ways of Sodom with them.

Lot had put self ahead of even his own family. These two girls he had offered to the men of the town, and their carnal natures were not slow to respond to the lustful suggestion. It is easier to grow weeds than flowers, and Lot had planted a heavy crop.

Verse 31: Our father is old, and there is not a man

One generation always seems old to the next generation. But here is the cry of two girls who have been deprived of everything they had a right to expect from life, because their father had followed his own will instead of God's will. If he had gone

171

God's way, he would have lived in peace with Abraham and would have found husbands for his daughters among the many servants of Abraham. They would have had an honored place, and Lot could have become a man of influence in Abraham's camp. His four hundred armed servants, their wives and families would have brought the total of Abraham's retainers up to several thousand. But Lot wanted none of this and as a result he wrecked his daughters' chances, and ended his life in horrible shame and sorrow.

Verse 32: Let us make our father drink
Only one of the commandments has a promise attached: "Honor thy father and thy mother." Although the commandments were not given at the time of Lot, the principle is certainly inherent in the human race and finds its highest expression in some Oriental countries where filial piety is the heart of religion.

Many children have made shipwreck of their lives because they would not submit to their parents. There can be no true blessing from God for any individual who fails to give filial respect to parents. Parents must pray for their children and lead them to Christ; children must honor their parents and pray for them.

Verse 33: The first-born went in
Sometimes unsaved people criticize the Bible because of its horrible stories of all varieties of iniquity: murder, adultery, rape, incest, treason, high crimes, and foul deeds. But these things are never mentioned without being accompanied by the stern warning that God hates sin and punishes it. It is far better for children to learn the facts of life from the Word of God where sin is condemned than from dirty words on alley walls, or from lewd stories. No one can escape knowledge of sin, but anyone can be protected from the power of sin by being encompassed in Christ.

He perceived not
Here is an example of two sorts of blindness. Drink can intoxicate a man so that he is blind to events in which he is an active participant. He loses his self-control and acts according

to the roots of sin in his heart and not according to the branches which he has cultivated before men.

Far greater blindness, however, is the general blindness of sin which encompasses the whole world, and lurks in the old heart of the truly saved man. Here is proof that God Himself never changes the old heart, but condemns it and gives the believer a new heart. The unsaved man lives in blindness but Jesus came that the blind might see, and that those who think themselves sighted might be made blind (John 9:39-41).

Verse 34: The first-born said unto the younger

We are all inclined to look up to older people. As babies we learn from those who are older; as children we learn much from those who are only slightly older than we are. But when we are older, we are the examples of the younger and must do all we can to influence them for Christ. Eliab lost the throne to David because God saw his heart (I Samuel 16:7); he did not have a proper attitude toward his younger brother (I Samuel 17:28).

Lot's daughter influenced the younger to commit sin. She was the dominating spirit and the ringleader in the depravity which they practiced. Both had been promised in marriage but were evidently very young, as they had not yet lived with their husbands (verse 8). Both were guilty but the older sister was much more guilty.

Verse 36: By their father

Christ taught us, that without Him we can do nothing (John 15:5). But God teaches us here that believers who get out of the will of God and produce fruit by their own efforts must be judged by God. That which is born of the flesh is always flesh (John 3:6). It is possible for a preacher to preach an incestuous sermon. He may not perceive that he has done it, even as Lot did not know, but the fruit was there.

Any man who works in the energy of the flesh will impregnate a congregation with a type of religion that is devoid of true spiritual power. A Christian man may have this type of life in his home, or may teach this kind of thing to his Sunday school class. The whole of life may be the effluvia of a corpse instead of the holy breath of the living Spirit.

Verses 37, 38: Moab . . . Ammon . . .

"Let no one say when he is tempted 'I am tempted by God'; for God cannot be tempted with evil and he himself tempts no one; but each person is tempted when he is lured and enticed by his own desire. Then desire when it has conceived gives birth to sin; and sin when it is full-grown brings forth death. Do not be deceived, my beloved brethren" (James 1:13-16, RSV). Lot's life perfectly illustrates this verse. Lot was tempted by the pasture land near Sodom. Then in the shadow of the city he conceived the idea of living in Sodom. The consequences of Sodom were Moab and Ammon. It was a chain reaction of sin.

Unto this day

Hundreds of years afterward, the children of Moab and Ammon opposed the march of Israel from Egypt to Canaan. Balak, king of Moab, secured Balaam's services to curse the people of God (Numbers 22:5). Near Moab was Edom, the country of the children of Esau. Thus a quartet of infamy plagued the children of God through all their history: Abraham's Ishmael; Isaac's Esau; and Lot's Moab and Ammon. From these comes the Arab race of today and the religion of Islam, the greatest barrier in the progress of Christian missions and to Israel's possession of the land. Thus the fruit of our flesh opposes the fruit of the Spirit.

Genesis 20

Verse 1: Abraham journeyed from thence . . . and dwelled . . . and sojourned in Gerar

Why will a man who has lived in the presence of the Lord leave his place of high privilege for the barren wastes of self-will? A Christian can move from victory to triumph to sin and defeat. Abraham left God for Gerar. God wanted Abraham to stay by the altar where his tent was pitched and where God had blessed him.

Verse 2: Abraham said of Sarah his wife, she is my sister

The man of faith has no right to deceive the world around him. If Sarah had been only Abraham's sister, any man in the land would have had the right to seek an honorable union with her. But because of this lie, the Philistine took something that was not his right. A lie is never justifiable, even to save a life. No matter how men may argue about it, the divine principle has been established, and nothing can change it. Abraham lied to protect his own life. True love would have made Abraham willing to sacrifice his life for Sarah.

There is no good in man, no matter how far he may have advanced with the Lord. Anything that is good in any man is that which comes from the Lord, and all that is wrong comes from the man. Abraham had the nature of Adam, and so have we.

Abimelech . . . sent, and took Sarah

It was no chance or coincidence in this fact that Sarah fell into the hands of an alien king for the second time. After Egypt, Abimelech.

Satan, of course, was making war on God. He knew that the promised seed of the woman would come through Abraham and Sarah. Satan who had sought to pollute the race with demons before the flood was now seeking to pollute the womb of Sarah. He works on in undying enmity against the seed of the woman.

Verse 3: God came to Abimelech in a dream

God is a God of great grace. Though Abimelech was an unconscious transgressor against God's plan, he would have been punished, for ignorance is never an excuse with God. The grace of God here is extended even to a Gentile king. God condescends to warn him of his peril in order that he may escape the just judgment of God. Abimelech knows Him, not as Jehovah, the Redeemer, but as God, the Creator.

Thou art but a dead man

God threatened so severely because His faithfulness was at stake. No situation could have brought more dishonor on God's Messiah. A short while before, God had promised that Sarah would have the royal seed within a twelve-month. Suppose Abimelech had taken Sarah and God had not intervened? Two seeds would have been at the door to Sarah's womb, and to this day an element of doubt would cling to the ancestry of our Lord. Hence the heinousness of Abraham's and Sarah's deception of Abimelech becomes all the more apparent.

Verse 4: Abimelech had not come near her

God is jealous of His promises and surrounds them with such certainty that doubt is impossible. The child that Sarah would bear is Abraham's by supernatural vitalizing of both parents.

This detail about Abimelech reminds us of the story of the birth of our Lord, that Mary had not known a man (Luke 1:34), and that Joseph had never been with her (Matthew 1:18, 19). With such meticulous detail does God surround the story of redemption and the veracity of the record which He has given concerning His Son.

Lord, wilt thou slay also a righteous nation?

Abimelech addresses God as Master, not as Jehovah, Redeemer. He must have known of the recent destruction of

176

Sodom and Gomorrah, and perhaps approved it. But he recognized a vast difference between the morality of Gerar and the immorality of Sodom, and he pleads this difference as justification.

We must not be deceived by his false opinion. The Philistine nation was not righteous. If God spared Gerar, it was not because of any goodness in either its inhabitants or its king. The Lord withholds wrath because of His common grace, not because of any merit in man.

Verse 5: Said he not unto me

It is horrible to contemplate that sin of a believer may bring even death upon an unbeliever. One simple act provokes a chain of consequences. Abraham's unbelief degraded Sarah who merited his protection.

Her connivance tempted Abimelech and put him in danger. Because Abimelech stood as head of his people, judgment threatened them all. A preliminary warning of barrenness fell upon the women of his household (verses 17, 18), but now death threatened all that were with him (verse 7). And all of this began with the sin of the highest leader God had on earth. A Christian out of the will of God can spread spiritual infection to many that will have dire consequences.

Integrity . . . innocency . . .

It is regrettable that judged by human standards, many unregenerate people are more honorable than some believers. The name, Abimelech, means "father of a king." He is but the first of a long line of pagan moralists that includes Plato, Aristotle, Marcus Aurelius, and a host of others. Their moral height is so great that we are almost tempted to think of them as believers, but there is a great gulf fixed between them and us. They stand in another land, but they look across the abyss into our land and see truths that never belonged to them by nature and which are ours only through grace.

Verse 6: I know . . . I also withheld thee

There is nothing hid from God. The Creator had made Abimelech and knew his psychology. Abimelech acted honorably by the restraining power of God and not through following his natural proclivities. Abimelech already had a wife (verse 17) and had sent for Sarah to satisfy his fleshly desires. True, he

177

had a high code of morals like many unregenerate men, and probably would not have molested Sarah had he known that she was a wife and not an unattached sister.

But the providence of God was at work here for greater matters were at stake than the mere wife of a former Chaldean sheep-herder. God was protecting the line of the seed of the woman (Genesis 3:15). His promises would be fulfilled and His name remain unsullied.

Sinning against Me

To Abimelech is revealed a truth which David learned when he came back to God as a penitent. David sinned against Uriah by stealing his wife; he sinned against Bathsheba by causing her husband to be murdered; he sinned against the soldiers who had died in the futile attack which he commanded to be launched to do away with the unwanted husband; he sinned against the families of these men; he sinned against the nation whose king he was, and which he should have guided in righteousness.

But all this sin paled into insignificance when he considered that God was involved. So he cried out, "Against thee, thee only have I sinned, and done that which is evil in thy sight" (Psalm 51:4). This same truth here revealed to a pagan king is one of the most important in the Word of God.

Verse 7: Restore . . . for he is a prophet

Despite the sin of Abraham, God would not allow him to be dishonored in the eyes of the Philistine king. Abraham was not a prophet in the sense of one who announced the future, but in the etymological sense of one who stands out in front to represent God. For this he had been chosen out of the hole of the pit (Isaiah 51:2). God always takes care of those who are His. He defended Job against the counselors who darkened God's plan (sic Heb.) by words without knowledge (Job 38:2). And, amazing coincidence of names, when David "changed his behavior before that other Abimelech who drove him away" (Psalm 34:*title* cf. I Samuel 21), the Lord watched over David and vindicated him as the Psalm shows. By the very nature of His being, the Lord is bound to care for His own.

He shall pray for thee

Even before Abimelech's reproach and Abraham's feeble

178

defense, and unrecorded repentance, God announced that Abraham was His man, that Abraham would intercede and his prayer would be answered and Abimelech would be spared because of Abraham.

If we would only understand our high position as those who have been made accepted in the beloved (Ephesians 1:6), we would be more swift to return to the Lord when we fall into a state that is not acceptable to Him. For His hand is on us for good and He who began our salvation will carry it through to its uttermost fulfillment (Philippians 1:6). All of Christ's belong to God, and all of God's belong to Christ, and He is glorified in us (John 17:10). This gives us our place before God and the privilege of praying for others.

Verse 8: The men were sore afraid

The smell of Sodom's sulphur had blown away by this time, but it was still pungent in the nostrils of memory. God who can exercise such judgment as that which fell upon the cities of the plain, can strike terror to the hearts of the Philistines. And when the man who is the friend of that God comes around, it is well to treat him and all his household most circumspectly, even though they come with lies and enticements that could cause death to the whole community. And perhaps it would be best to say that they are to be treated circumspectly *especially* when they use deceit. For when there is deviation from the straight line with God, He is bound to make the crooked places straight.

Verse 9: Abimelech called Abraham

It was a shameful moment for Abraham. There is nothing pretty about the sight of this old man who had just had such lofty experiences, being called to account by a petty Philistine king. It was bad enough that a justified believer, a prophet of God, should be reproved at all by this pagan king, but the disgrace is all the greater, since Abraham was totally responsible for it, and deserved the humiliation. It wasn't as though he had been caught off guard. He was guilty of a lie that had been well-rehearsed and which had already sent him out of Egypt like a cur with his tail between his legs.

What hast thou done unto us?

This question many unsaved people put to Christians who

fail to witness to them. Members of women's clubs will one day ask the believers why they considered making five no trumps more important than bringing them life eternal. Businessmen will one day ask their believing associates why they so lived as to give the impression that making money was more important than telling a soul of eternal life.

Abraham should have witnessed to the Philistines, since all families were promised blessing through him (12:3). Instead, he lived the great lie of a life that did not acknowledge the dominion of his Lord in all things.

Thou hast brought . . . a great sin

If Abimelech had bitterly reproached Abraham, it would have been only what the patriarch deserved, but the king comports himself with the utmost dignity, and seems to be sincerely and profoundly shocked by the episode.

Verse 10: What sawest thou

Surely Abraham had no evidence to go on. His was evidently a suspicious nature. To say the least Abraham was uncharitable. He believed he was among a people who would kill to satisfy their lust.

We might excuse him if we had not found him already guilty of a similar unkindness toward the Egyptians. We have no right to judge those whom we do not know. We are to be examples of love, and love bears all things, believes all things, hopes all things (I Corinthians 13:7).

Verse 11: Abraham said

Abraham should have said, "Forgive me, Abimelech, for dishonoring both you and my God. My selfish cowardice overwhelmed me, and I denied my God by fearing that He who called me could not take care of me. He is not as your gods of wood and stone. He is the God of glory. He is the living God, the Creator, the most High God, possessor of heaven and earth. He told me He would be my shield and my exceeding great reward, and supplier of all my needs. Never has any child of Adam sinned against so much grace. In sinning against Him, I sinned against you. Forgive me, Abimelech."

Because I thought

We shall always be in trouble if we do our own thinking instead of relying on the revelation of God. "The Lord knows the thoughts of man, that they are but a breath" (Psalm 94:11, RSV). An old Scotch lady said, "I have learned that in the long run the Almighty is generally correct."

David said, "I have laid up thy word in my heart, that I might not sin against thee" (Psalm 119:11, RSV). If Abraham had hidden in his heart the revelations that God had given him, he would not have fallen into this sin.

Surely the fear of God is not in this place

It wasn't even in Abraham! There is never any excuse for sin, certainly none for Abraham's sin. Abraham had proved the faithfulness and loving-kindness of God for almost forty years, and had recently received the most definite promises concerning the purposes of God. God had supped with him and had talked with him as His friend. Every sin is against the grace of God and His loving care for us.

They will slay me

Personal cowardice is never pleasant to contemplate. Fool-hardy boldness is more attractive than a craven timidity that will risk the safety of a tender loved one for one's personal security. Abraham was the father of all who believe; surely all of his children have been guilty of this same lack of trust in God.

God dealt sternly with Israel in the wilderness because of their sin against the knowledge of His loving care. God smote the rock and waters gushed out, and the people immediately said, "Can he also give bread, or provide meat for his people?" Then was God angry with Israel "Because they had no faith in God, and did not trust his saving power. . . . They tested him again and again, and provoked the Holy One of Israel" (Psalm 78:20, 22, 41, RSV).

Verse 12: Indeed she is my sister

Can this be noble Abraham, groveling around, shifty-eyed and mealy-mouthed? When put to the test, even the best of all the saints are just as liable to fall through their inherent weakness. All are weak and fallible, and God wishes us to learn that we are to fix our gaze upon Him, and not on any man. "Let anyone who thinks that he stands take heed lest he fall" (I Corinthians 10:12, RSV).

Verse 13: When God caused me to wander

There is a terrible meaning in this verb "wander" which Abraham uses. The Hebrew word occurs exactly fifty times in Scripture and never in a good sense. It is used of animals going astray, of a drunken man reeling, or staggering, of sinful seduction, of a prophet's lies causing the people to err, of the path of a lying heart. Six other words are translated "wander," any one of which Abraham might have used, but he used the worst word available.

One of the terrible fruits of sin is that it casts the blame back upon God. Adam said, "The woman *thou* gavest me. . . ." And Abraham here shows the traits inherited from Adam. Such things can happen in a man to whom the God of glory has appeared and who has walked with God for forty years.

I said unto her

Abraham himself had originated this deception of sin, and the horrible fact now emerges that it had not been practiced for almost forty years.

The continuing power of evil in the lives of believers is evident both from what we find in ourselves and from what we see in Scripture. The notion that the old nature can be eradicated is alien to the Word of God. Paul confessed that in himself, in his flesh, there was no good thing (Romans 7:18). Well on in his Christian life, Abraham revealed here his foul nature that after all these years was still hankering after its own ways, looking to its own power for protection.

This is thy kindness which thou shalt shew unto me

A lie is never a kindness. Nothing gained by sin is worth the price paid for it. Here was the view of the natural man, since we discover that this agreement with Sarah was made in Ur of the Chaldees before Abraham knew God. The terrible thing is that such unregenerate thoughts slip out into the open and claim to be truth, even as a counterfeit always claims to be real.

This is what the New Testament calls "The deceitfulness of sin," and why the Holy Spirit exhorts us, "Take care, brethren, lest there be in any of you an evil, unbelieving heart, leading

182

you to fall away from the living God. But exhort one another every day as long as it is called 'today,' that none of you may be hardened by the deceitfulness of sin" (Hebrews 3:12, 13, RSV). The hardening power of deceit is shown by the fact that dear old Father Abraham makes this horrible confession in extenuation of the evil he has done.

Say . . . he is my brother

The fact that Sarah had no children helped her to exploit this lie. It saved her face somewhat, since barrenness was considered a disgrace, but it led to sin upon sin. This agreement was to be carried out "in every place," and we do not know in how many places besides Egypt and Gerar the farce was played.

The double role of wife and sister suited the pride of Sarah and quelled the fears of Abraham. Early in their "wandering" they took out this mortgage of sin, and the enemy was able to foreclose on demand. What an illustration of the fact that it is our own selfish interests which cause us to depart from God!

Verse 14: Abimelech took sheep

The Philistine king is now heaping coals of fire upon the head of Abraham. The latter should have given Abimelech a large present and gone on his way. But the pagan king, innocent victim of deception, makes the present to Abraham.

It is indeed sad when an unregenerate man rebukes a believer, because it is so evident that the believer knew what was right and did not do it. Instead of being a blessing to others, he becomes a temptation; instead of giving to their need, he receives from their bounty. It must have been a bitter pill, but Abraham should have swallowed it without water.

Verse 16: Thus she was reproved

Whether or not Sarah as Abraham's partner in the deception had to suffer the consequences and endure the reproof from the man whom she had so nearly wronged, we do not know. Abraham was given the permission to dwell where he desired, but there was a money gift that was to be spent for veils for Sarah and all her attendants, that they might no longer tempt Abimelech's subjects by their beauty. The Hebrew reads that it was the gift that was to be the covering. It may also mean that it was a propitiation, an attempt to cover the sin. This would indeed be a rebuke if Abimelech thought that Sarah had no sacrifice which could be presented to God for her sin.

Verse 17: Abraham prayed

If he had prayed for himself before going into Abimelech's country, Abraham would not have had to ask God to undo the sin he had committed. But here the power of the covenant shines out in splendor. The man who was sinned against was chastised, and the man who committed the sin became the intercessor. What striking evidence that no man can approach God except through the covenant of grace which is in the Lord Jesus Christ!

Seemingly righteous Abimelech was afflicted and seemingly unrighteous Abraham was blessed, restored and given power in prayer. The sovereign grace of God shines out with brilliance. Works certainly do not enter into this transaction. If there had been a condition involved in the call of Abraham, it would have been broken by now, but God worked according to His own sovereign choice, and His own purpose, and in that Abraham was complete.

Verse 18: Because of Sarah Abraham's wife

It is seldom that we can counteract the results of sin which we have committed, but here God honored His servant's intercession. God tells us that "The prayer of a righteous man has great power in its effects" (James 5:16, RSV). The righteousness is not in the man but in Christ. The covenant was with Abraham, and thus touched his wife. For her sake, God moved to punish a whole tribe, even though they were innocent from a human point of view.

What an incentive for us to pray for those who have been hurt through some action of ours, for, even though they are innocent they suffer because they have touched someone who is in a covenant relationship with God through Christ.

184

Genesis 21

Verse 1: As He had said . . . as He had spoken

God is a God of His word. If He were not, the universe would fall apart. The long-awaited child would never have been born if God had not acted. Isaac, we are told in the New Testament illustrates the covenant of grace (Galatians 4:28). We are born, "not of blood, nor of the will of the flesh, nor of the will of man but of God" (John 1:13). "Of his own will begat he us by the word of truth, that we should be a kind of first-fruits of his creatures" (James 1:18).

We never could have saved ourselves any more than Abraham could have begotten a son in his own strength. The life of God must come to us in salvation even as it came upon Sarah. The birth of eternal life within us is a virgin birth: that is, as the Spirit overshadowed the body of sinful Mary and begat the sinless Christ in her, so the Spirit comes upon unregenerate man and begets new life within.

Verse 2: Sarah conceived, and bare

The first line we ever read about Sarah was that she was barren and that she had no child (11:30). We remember that when she heard that she would have a child in a year she laughed, and that the Lord rebuked her for it (18:12-14). She was ninety years old, and had every right to laugh from a human point of view.

But faith looks at things not from the human point of view but through God's eyes. Since we read in the New Testament that it was through faith that Sarah received strength to conceive seed, and since the conception took place three months after the announcement that she greeted with laughter, we can see that a ninety-year-old woman moved from doubt to faith in three months.

A son in his old age, at the set time

The steps by which God brought Abraham to this moment were wonderful especially in their typical meaning. Abraham was a man of faith, but even faith must learn that it is but the channel, and not the source of blessing. During the years when Abraham had procreative power, even though he had Ishmael, he could not produce Isaac, for the latter represents the life of grace which bears fruit only after the flesh has been crucified.

Self-will is no longer considered a means to bring a promise to fulfillment. Death and deadness are recognized, but they no longer obstruct true faith. Isaac, the type of laughter and joy, is born, and he is in the line of the promised seed. God is never ahead of His time and He never lags behind. Whatever He promises comes to pass at the right moment.

Verse 2: Isaac

It is a great thing to obey God. Abraham might have refused to give his beloved son a name that carried memories of early doubt. But God chooses a name in order to give it a meaning that will transcend our thoughts in beauty and wonder. God was going to bring a blessing through Isaac that would turn the laughter of doubt to the shout of triumph. This was as great as the change indicated by substituting for Simon, a wishy-washy character, the name of Peter, which means "rock."

God never does anything by halves. Take a handful of pebbles, scatter them away and you get Jezreel, a name given to Isaac's descendants when they were scattered (Hosea 1:4). Take a handful of wheat and sow it, and you are planting, which is the meaning of Jezreel when God restores His people to the land (Hosea 1:11).

Verse 6: God hath made me to laugh

Anything that God does is well done. Sarah could have sung the 126th Psalm. "When the Lord turned again the barrenness of Sarah, I was like them that dream. Then was my mouth filled with laughter, and my tongue with singing." This old woman suddenly found herself with child; her laughter became one of joy and satisfaction. Her condition was almost too good to be true. Then the child was in her arms, and at her breast, and she found herself a mother after a life of barrenness. Furthermore, she knew that it had all been done by the power of God.

All that hear will laugh with me

The 126th Psalm which Sarah could have sung has a verse for those who stand by and see what the Lord has done; "Then they said among the nations, 'The Lord has done great things for them'" (v. 2, RSV). Thus we may rejoice with Sarah and say, "The Lord has done great things for Sarah." We can grow in the Lord so that those who live around us will be forced to join in the testimony to the goodness and the power of our God.

Verse 7: Who would have said unto Abraham

The amazed and almost incredulous delight of the old lady is beautiful to contemplate. Doubtless she squeezed little Isaac so tightly that he cried, and then covered him with kisses. Whoever would have dreamed of such a thing? Laughter! Laughter! My little baby, Laughter! Whoever would have said it?

God Himself quotes a verse in Isaiah and applies it to Sarah's joy. "Rejoice, O barren one that dost not bear; break forth and shout, thou who are not in travail; for the desolate hath more children than she who hath a husband" (Isaiah 54:1; Galatians 4:27, RSV).

Verse 8: And the child grew, and was weaned

In the East this takes place at a much later date than in our land. Isaac was probably three to five years old when he was weaned (cf. Matthew 21:16).

As newborn babes we should desire the sincere milk of the word, that we may grow thereby (I Peter 2:2), but God tells us that we must be weaned to the diet of an adult believer. "But solid food is for the mature, for those who have their faculties trained by practice to distinguish good from evil" (Hebrews 5:14, RSV). "Whom will he teach knowledge and to whom will he explain the message? Those who are weaned

187

from the milk, those taken from the breast" (Isaiah 28:9, RSV).

Abraham made a great feast

It is an occasion for feasting when a baby Christian learns to eat, grows into the meat of the Word and is assured of his justification and security. It is a cause for celebration when a believer is no longer preoccupied with elementary doctrines, but enters into the deep truths of the Word of God.

It is profoundly significant that the first verse of the sixth chapter of Hebrews follows the last verse of the fifth chapter. If the chapter break is removed it will be understood what weaning means. The one who has left milk (Hebrews 5:13) for meat (Hebrews 5:14), has left the primary doctrines (6:1, 2), and will know that the apostasy (6:4-6) could never be the lot of a justified man (6:9). The weaned child lives on grace alone.

Verse 9: Sarah saw the son of Hagar

No communion is possible between Ishmael and Isaac. One is the son of a slave, the other the son of the free woman. The former is the child of Abraham's natural powers, the latter is the child of God's miraculous intervention in grace.

We are told in Galatians that the two boys — though historical — are an allegory of the Old Testament and the New. Up to the time of Isaac's birth, Ishmael, in the eyes of the world, held succession to the father's estate. But the birth of Isaac changed everything. Ishmael represents human effort which is opposed to the free gift of God. If grace is to reign, law must be removed.

Mocking

The New Testament interprets this word as *persecuting*. "But as at that time he who was born according to the flesh persecuted him who was born according to the Spirit, so it is now" (Galatians 4:29, RSV). The flesh cannot tolerate grace. The flesh hates grace. This is why even some Christians positively hate the idea of salvation as being by grace. The world does not hate us because we believe in moral reform, but because we say that we were chosen by God in grace alone (John 15:19).

Any Christian who does not hold the doctrine of security of the believer is an Ishmael who has not allowed the flesh to be

188

cast out in order that the child of the free woman may reign supreme.

Verse 10: Cast out this bond woman and her son

Sin always produces chain reaction. Sarah's sin had produced envy, jealousy, and strife, and now it is to produce, from the human point of view, an act of cruelty. Hagar was not responsible for being a slave, and she had no choice when her body was given to Abraham. She had borne the child at Sarah's suggestion, and in her slave-mentality, could not help being proud of what she had done. Sarah could not tolerate being despised by Hagar nor could she tolerate seeing her son mocked by Ishmael. Domestic harmony was destroyed by the very means Sarah had employed to achieve happiness. It is impossible to have joy in any way but God's way.

The son of this bond woman shall not be heir with my son

If we see in Sarah's action only the venting of spleen, we miss the point of the story. Sarah had tolerated the slave woman and her son for some eighteen years. Now they must go. When we are weaned and have advanced in understanding of spiritual truth, we shall understand that the seed of Hagar rises against the seed of Sarah.

As long as Ishmael was alone, his nature was undetected, but when he was in contrast to the child of grace, he not only despised, but mocked and persecuted God's Isaac. "Isaac, though mocked, is the heir; and his coming casts out that which had hitherto occupied the house of faith."

Verse 11: The thing was very grievous in Abraham's sight

It is understandable that Abraham should love Ishmael, who, for many years had been his only son, the light and joy of his heart. Abraham genuinely loved Hagar, and this in no wise detracts from the fact that he genuinely loved Sarah. The exclusiveness of woman's love was a part of the curse (Genesis 3:16), but it was not put upon man. This has determined much of the flow of human history. Abraham probably knew Sarah well enough to detect her littleness which was a contributing factor in her jealousy. He probably thought that a less severe remedy would accomplish the desired effect. He wanted to hold on to his love of the flesh. But it had to go.

Verse 12: In all that Sarah hath said unto thee, hearken unto her voice

There are times when a man must listen to his wife, because the Lord has given her a quick discernment and an intuition which transcends a man's ability to make a rapid appraisal. At a glance, one woman can accurately estimate the cost of another woman's clothes, and analyze her character and personality. It takes a man much longer to acquire the same information.

In Isaac shall thy seed be called

God goes back to His original covenant promise. Events will pass in accordance with the eternal plan. Not the child of fleshly effort is to be the heir, but the miracle child of grace. It could not be otherwise. This is plainly revealed in the New Testament. The stories of Cain and Abel, of Isaac and Ishmael, and of Jacob and Esau illustrate the true nature of the brotherhood of man. The principles upon which these brothers acted animated the entire human race.

We may be sure that the same violent reactions will surge forth whenever circumstances set the stage for their performance. God will bless only through grace and the world, the flesh and the devil hate grace.

Verse 13: Also of the son of the bond woman

God promised Abraham that Ishmael also would become a great nation. The ways of God are past finding out (Romans 11:33). For hundreds of years, Ishmael has been in the land of Israel, blocking the return of Isaac. The Arabs are there today, bitterly hating the Jews, even as Ishmael hated Isaac. But never forget that they are a nation because God promised Abraham that He would make Ishmael a nation also.

Because he is thy seed

Ishmael, the fruit of Sarah's pique and Abraham's easy weakness was to be cast out; he could not be accepted by God to head the line of the Messiah, but he would be blessed and would become a nation. Why? Because he was a child of Abraham. This tender verse shows what God will do for a friend. God chose to bless Ishmael, not because of anything in this mocking wild-ass man, but because he was the child of Abraham.

190

Here the covenant of grace is at work in a remarkable way. God made promises to Abraham, and He is going to keep them. Nothing that man can do can alter the certainty of the divine Word. God has sworn by Himself and it shall come to pass. Though Ishmael mocks, yet God abides faithful. He cannot deny Himself.

Verse 14: Bread and a bottle of water

Could not a man so rich as Abraham have given them meat, and cakes made of fine flour? He was deeply grieved the night before, but now he rose early in the morning and sent them away. The Lord had given divine approval of Sarah's demand, so he was acting according to God's instructions.

Even though God promises to make a great nation of Ishmael for Abraham's sake, it is not through any merit of Ishmael, for Ishmael has no claim on God, or Abraham. Even the commonest blessings are given by God.

Putting it on her shoulder

Could not Abraham have spared one ass out of all his herds? It must have been an affectionate and touching farewell, but Abraham was stedfast in his obedience to the Lord.

The New Testament reveals the astounding significance of this farewell. Hagar represents Mt. Sinai, the law, and the law must be cast out before grace can triumph. This ancient family quarrel is recorded by God in meticulous detail to teach us that the legalists must always hate the children of grace, and that the former must be cast out by the latter.

And sent her away

There was no other solution. God will not allow grace to be mocked by the law. Legalism must be cleansed from the life of every believer if there is to be vigor and great joy. The New Testament makes this clear: "But as at that time he who was born according to the flesh persecuted him who was born according to the Spirit, so it is now" (Galatians 4:29). The implications of the contrast between the *then* and the *now* in that verse are very important.

Indeed, the carnal man today cannot endure that any persons should be marked by God as His favored and peculiar people. The very name "saints" and "elect" are as offensive to this world as that of Isaac was to Ishmael, because it imports a preference in the Father's estimation of the sons of grace.

Verse 16: Let me not see the death of the child

What total lack of faith in the heart of Hagar! When she earlier fled from Sarah, God told Hagar that He would multiply her descendants exceedingly, so that they could not be numbered for multitude (16:10). She should have believed the promise, but she represents law and legalism can never comprehend the life of grace through faith. How different was the same promise received by the father of her child! Abraham considered the deadness of his body, and the deadness of Sarah's womb and disregarded both. He looked at death and saw life. Hagar looked at her living son and saw death.

Verse 17: What aileth thee Hagar?

To complain against the providences of God is one facet of the sin of unbelief. It pervades the whole human race. It is found in the godly, no less than in the ungodly. God had told Hagar before Ishmael was born that He would take care of her and her son. To whine because circumstances are difficult is to doubt the Word of God. To suggest that the lad might die is to deny the Word of God.

Verse 19: A well of water . . . filled the bottle with water

Isaac lived his life near wells. Ishmael lived in the desert and did not know there was a well nearby until God showed it to Hagar. Even then he drank only from skins, for Ishmael represents the legalist; he can never have the joy of the child of grace, who draws water from the wells of salvation (Isaiah 12:3).

Whether or not Ishmael will be in heaven, we do not know, but there are multitudes of professing Christians like him. They live in a dry land, they cannot draw for themselves, and when their skins of water are empty, they are faint, until someone else fills it up for them. But still they live in a thirsty land and ultimately must give way to those who live by the wells of grace.

Verse 20: An archer

The child of grace has the sword as his weapon. Ishmael, child of bondage, was one with Nimrod and Esau, the archers

192

who sorely grieve Joseph, who shoot at him and hate him because he dwells by the well, and because his fruitful branches run over the wall (Genesis 49:22, 23). Despite the enmity of the archers for those who dwell by the wells, we, the children of grace, shall not be afraid of the arrows that fly by day (Psalm 91:5).

Verse 21: Him a wife out of the land of Egypt

Legalism always ends in marriage with the world. Egypt was the child of Ham who was cursed. The slave woman's child inherits a promise because of the paternity in Abraham, but this child takes after the mother. That which is born of the flesh can never be other than flesh (John 3:6).

That is why we are not to be in an unequal yoke with unbelievers. What fellowship can there be between a believer with two natures and an unbeliever with only one nature? Hagar "bearing children for slavery" (Galatians 4:24), and having brought forth an archer, she gets an Egyptian to be his wife. Thus legalism hates grace and moves toward the world.

Verse 22: God is with thee in all that thou doest

It is impossible for a believer to walk with God without the world noticing the power of God in his life. The Philistine world takes cognizance of the power and presence of the true God in the life of Abraham. This incident occurs while Abraham is living the ordinary humdrum life.

On such ordinary days, God can be manifest and magnified in the life of a believer. Abimelech had heard of the birth of Isaac, and understood that this was a miracle of nature. The world must marvel, and take knowledge that the believer has been with Jesus (Acts 4:13).

Verse 23: Swear unto me here by God

Abimelech had reason to scorn Abraham who had proved himself a liar and a coward. But Isaac has been born to Abraham and Sarah who were past age, and Abimelech immediately seeks peace for himself, his household and his land. Perhaps he has become afraid of Abraham, for it is awesome to know a man to whom God subjected kings, a man whom God warned of the destruction of cities, delivered him from his follies and to whom he gave a child after the usual age of reproduction. It is best to be at peace with such a man, so he makes a solemn treaty with Abraham. The world has long since learned to seek blessings at the heels of the blessed.

Verse 24: I will swear

Abraham was ready to accede to the request of the heathen king. The believer is to be a man of peace where no compromise is involved. The New Testament teaches us that we are to "Conduct yourself wisely toward outsiders" (Colossians 4:5, RSV); that we are to "command the respect of outsiders" (I Thessalonians 4:12, RSV), and that we are to "be well thought of by outsiders" (I Timothy 3:7, RSV).

God is concerned that we shall so live that the world will comprehend that we have His grace and favor, and that we are the objects of His love and care. Abraham's readiness to meet every desire of Abimelech showed that he was indeed a man of peace, and that he meant no ill whatsoever toward the unbeliever.

Verse 25: And Abraham reproved Abimelech

The believer may make a covenant with an unbeliever, but he must protest any attempt to touch his wells. Water is a symbol of the Word of God, and man is not to live by bread alone but by every word that proceeds out of the mouth of God (Deuteronomy 8:3; Matthew 4:4). Too often the world will desire to make a covenant with us and will then proceed to attack our water supply — the Word of God. Abraham saw the danger at once and reproved his host for this breach of trust.

The Christian must be aware that he cannot walk and work with anyone who seeks to contaminate his belief in the supreme authority of the Scripture. Here are the springs of our spiritual life. We can no more countenance an attack on our source of water than we can permit slow draining of our blood.

Verse 27: Abraham took sheep and oxen

Although Abraham was the one to be compensated, we find him offering a gift instead. "And the Lord's servant must not be quarrelsome but kindly to every one, an apt teacher, forbearing, correcting his opponents with gentleness" (II Timothy 2:24, 25, RSV). The world is usually truculent, the believer must be conciliatory. Abraham did not compromise on the es-

194

sential points of difference, but he was conciliatory on all the points that affected peaceable relations.

Verse 29: What mean these seven ewe lambs?

It was customary to exchange presents at the time of the making of a solemn covenant. Asa reminded Ben-hadad of a covenant between their respective fathers, and asserted that the covenant was binding because he had sent a present of silver and gold to the Syrian king (I Kings 15:19). Ephraim sent oil to Egypt in token of that unholy alliance (Hosea 12:1). What astonished Abimelech was that Abraham provided seven ewe lambs as a gift beyond the covenant gift.

The Christian goes the second mile (Matthew 5:41). He is to provide things honest in the sight of all men. The Greek of Romans 12:17 is that we are to provide things beautiful, or attractive, in the sight of all men. The Lord has no representative upon this earth other than the redeemed.

Verse 30: A witness unto me that I have digged this well

Faith never allows itself to be deprived of its fruit. The world must never be allowed to claim that it is the source of our blessing and our supply. The lambs were a witness that Abimelech had no claim on the waters that poured forth to Abraham.

The warfare of works against faith is most subtle, and will never know an armistice. Continually the flesh seeks credit for the blessing of the believer. We shall always be presenting our ewe lambs to witness against the flesh. The well of salvation is the work of grace; the world and the flesh must deserve no credit for the fruits of grace.

Verse 31: Beersheba

This place has been identified several miles southwest of Hebron. It was on the boundary of the occupied land. Like the phrase, "From Maine to California," from Dan to Beersheba indicated the limits of the kingdom. Beersheba means either "the well of the seven" or "the well of the oath." The two words in Hebrew are connected etymologically. Archaeologists have actually discovered seven wells at the place identified as Beersheba.

After the covenant was made and presents given, Abimelech

and Phicol returned to Philistia and Abraham remained in full possession of the well. The world does not long keep fellowship with the true Christian. The uneasiness caused by his presence drives the unbeliever away. Abraham retains possession of the well.

Verse 33: The name of the Lord, the everlasting God

Abraham has learned many names of God up to this point, and now comes another. The God of glory had appeared to him; he had some knowledge of Jehovah, he had met *El Elyon,* the most High God, possessor of heaven and earth; he had found God as his shield and exceeding great reward; he had met *El Shaddai,* the nourisher and supplier. Now, after long pursuit of the daily round, he calls upon God as *El Olam,* the God of the successive ages.

Verse 34: Abraham sojourned . . . many days

We must learn to live life one day at a time. It is the long stretch that tires us. If we seek to live out of the moment, we shall be spiritually wearied. A woman once told me that in ten years she had calculated that she would sweep 4,672,000 square feet of floor space in her five room home. She had reached the figure by measuring the house, finding that it had 1,280 square feet and multiplying the figure by 365 and then by 10! I suppose the number of plates, cups, saucers, pots and pans to be washed in ten years could reach a staggering total. I told her, however, that she would never work more than one day at a time. That is true of all of life, whether it be the living through hours of high fever or lone nights of suffering and sleeplessness.

Genesis 22

Verse 1: After these things, God did tempt Abraham

This does not mean, of course, that God enticed Abraham toward sin. It means that one could be drawn upward or downward. Little by little the latter direction captured the whole word. God says, "Let no one say when he is tempted [downward], 'I am tempted by God'; for God cannot be tempted with evil and he himself tempts no one" (James 1:13, RSV).

Verse 2: Take thy son, thine only son Isaac

This is one of the Bible's blessed contradictions. There are no real contradictions, but several are planned by God to teach us deep truth. After spending a chapter on Ishmael and recording Abraham's cry, "Oh that Ishmael might live in thy sight" (17:18), God now calls Isaac Abraham's only son. The New Testament says that Abraham offered up "his only son" (Hebrews 11:17). Here is an only son who had a brother! God is showing us a pageant, a type, a parable of the heavenly Father offering up His only begotten Son.

We read of "Hamlet, Prince of Denmark." So in his pageant it is "Abraham, the Father," and "Isaac, the only son." God so loved the world that He gave His Isaac.

Get thee into the land of Moriah

Moriah means "chosen by God," and it became the site of the temple where all the sacrifices were offered, and where God rent the veil in two that free access might be for all the people of God. We read in Chronicles, "Then Solomon began to build the house of the Lord in Jerusalem on Mount Moriah, where the Lord had appeared to David his father, at the place that David had appointed, on the threshing floor of Ornan the Jebusite" (II Chronicles 3:1, RSV).

In Abraham's day it was uninhabited. Abraham could not see Jerusalem, the temple and Calvary, but the Lord God saw them. Not only was Christ the Lamb slain from the foundation of the world (Revelation 13:8), and His people chosen from the foundation of the world (Ephesians 1:4), but Calvary was designated as the place.

Offer him there for a burnt offering

Though God was telling Abraham to offer up Isaac, He knew in advance that He intended to provide a lamb for a substitute, and that Isaac would walk down the hill alive with his father. Ishmael was not offered but cast out. Isaac must be offered as a sacrifice.

Legal works are never acceptable to God, but the sacrifice provided and demanded by God is indeed acceptable to Him. Abraham would walk up the mount with Isaac, but he would come down with Isaac and a much greater knowledge of God.

Verse 3: Abraham rose up early in the morning

God has issued a command, and the response to His command must be obedience. And the synonymn of true obedience is true faith. Abraham believed God, and was therefore ready to obey, even to offer up what was most dear. He must make the sacrifice in the place indicated by God. No explanation was given. He was called to believe and obey, and he did not hesitate for a moment. David describes such obedience, "I hasten and do not delay to keep thy commandments" (Psalm 119:60, RSV). Some commentators have pictured Abraham in silent agony, but there is no mention of anything but swift obedience.

Verse 4: On the third day

Of the many incidents in the Bible which took place on "third days," I have never found one that does not illustrate resurrection truth. The emphasis in this story is not on sacrifice or offering, but on receiving the most abundant grace of God. Abraham was not gloomy.

We believe he reckoned that God must perform a miracle

198

of resurrection. He had gotten Himself into a predicament by commanding the sacrifice of a son who according to His promise was to live and father a family. If Isaac had really died, God would have broken His promise. There can be no doubt that Abraham had calculated this, and expected resurrection (Hebrews 11:18, 19).

Abraham . . . saw the place afar off

His vision included more than a mountain in the land of Moriah. He saw past the deed to the resurrection, past the type to the fulfillment, past Isaac to the Lord Jesus Christ. The New Testament will not permit any other interpretation. He "considered that God was able to raise men even from the dead" (Hebrews 11:19, RSV), and thus began to see Christ's day. Our Lord reminded the Pharisees of this fact, "Your father Abraham rejoiced that he was to see my day; he saw it and was glad" (John 8:56, RSV).

Verse 5: I and the lad will go yonder and worship

It was not a heathen ritual of human sacrifice. Faith was stedfast, and saw the end from the beginning. By this time he was in such close friendship with God that he dwelt in joy. This is reflected throughout the narrative. The servants were not permitted to accompany them for they might have opposed the sacrifice of Isaac.

Faith must always go alone with God; it can never be accompanied by any alien presence. Thoughts which oppose the abandonment of the heart to God must be left behind when faith is crucified with Christ. Abraham had reached the stage of spiritual growth where every word and gesture are worship. His heart held nothing back.

I and the lad will . . . come again to you

Here is the flat announcement of Abraham's expectation. It is noteworthy that not a line describes Abraham's emotions. He had received certain promises which he was absolutely sure would be fulfilled to the last detail. He walked forward with the definite assurance that God was not a liar.

His strong faith is shown in his statement to the servants that Isaac would return with him. He truly believed that God intended Isaac would die, but he just as truly believed that

199

God would raise him from the dead, and that they would return.

Verse 6: Abraham took the wood of the burnt offering, and laid it upon Isaac his son

Abraham was exactly one hundred years older than Isaac. Was Isaac thirty-three? We do not know, but the Hebrew word which is translated *lad* is elsewhere used for armed soldiers. The point is that Isaac consented to be offered.

He was a true picture of Christ who said, "For this reason the Father loves me, because I lay down my life, that I may take it up again. No one takes it from me, but I lay it down of my own accord. I have power to lay it down, and I have power to take it again; this charge I have received from my Father" (John 10:17, 18, RSV). Abraham would have been no match for Isaac, if he had resisted, but Isaac bore the wood, as Christ bore the cross.

The fire in his hand, and the knife

We must die with Christ, and Abraham is experiencing this. The offering of Isaac is a much more significant picture of the cross than the lamb of Abel or the ark of Noah. Indeed, it speaks of the cross whereby we are crucified to the world and the world to us (Galatians 6:14).

Verse 7: Where is the lamb?

Isaac was fully aware that blood would have to be shed. In his mind there was already established the knowledge so necessary to every human being. We are sinners and sin means death. It means our own death or the death of a substitute. Abel took a lamb out of his flock, ready at hand. Noah was told to take two of every kind of animal into the ark, but to take seven pairs of clean animals for sacrifice. There were no lambs on Mount Moriah, only wild beasts, for a lamb would die unless taken care of by human beings.

Verse 8: God will provide himself a lamb

Every detail of the story shows that Abraham in firm faith was walking steadfastly to the place of sacrifice with the determination to obey God and to offer up his Isaac. His marvelous example of faith was that he obeyed without question and left all the details and the circumstances to God. As soon as we

200

know that God has spoken we must act upon the command to the full extent of our ability and leave the details to Him.

Verse 9: The place which God had told him of; and Abraham built an altar there

There was persistent determination in the faith of Abraham. God had given him this test of his love and obedience. There was no flinching but a steadfastness which amounted to dogged persistence. There is no wild dash ending in fatigue, but the slogging march of the infantryman. Day after day Abraham journeyed. On the third day he saw the place afar off (verse 4). Now he moved to accomplish his purpose and reached his goal. Not for one moment had he relaxed his determination to fulfill the divine command. This must characterize our walk of faith.

Now comes the final sacrifice, he is to offer his dearly beloved son, his only son. This did not deter him from gathering stones and building the altar. Bits of him had died before: the remainder was to die now in final obedience.

And laid the wood in order, and bound Isaac his son, and laid him on the altar

The wood was for the purpose of consuming the sacrifice. This line is a link in the chain of Bible revelation about the substitutionary sacrifice, and part of the evidence that God directed the details. He originally commanded the lamb, and evidently laid down the very method of offering it.

In Leviticus, where the continuing sacrifices are begun, we discover that pieces of wood were laid in order upon the altar (Leviticus 1:7), and that a horizontal bolt of fire from the Holy of Holies ignited the wood and consumed the offering (Leviticus 9:24). God Himself furnished the material and the fire consumed the sacrifice, for He Himself put His Son to death (Isaiah 53:10).

The glorious truth of this picture is that Isaac was a willing sacrifice. Abraham must have told him about his supernatural birth and of God's promise concerning him. Isaac now had a personal faith that was joined to that of Abraham.

Verse 10: Abraham . . . took the knife to slay his son

The center of the scene shifts from father to son and back to the father, for the Lord is emphasizing the fact that both were

201

going to the sacrifice together, obeying, yielding, cooperating, even as the heavenly Father and the Lord Jesus Christ did at Calvary.

With the consent of Isaac, Abraham binds him hand and foot, and lays him on the altar; then with confidence unshaken, and obedience unparalleled, he raises the knife to slay the victim. For in the heart of each was full devotion, though both expected death to strike, and fire to consume. The heart of the story is that both believed that out of the ashes God would bring forth resurrection life.

Verse 11: The angel of the Lord called unto him out of heaven

Only the intervention of God from heaven prevented the completion of this extraordinary act of faith. God had sufficiently tested the faith of His servant. Therefore, he stopped Abraham from dealing the death blow. God repudiated the heathen idea of a human sacrifice. Only when the Jews sank to the level of the heathen around them did they give their children to Moloch. Abraham offered to give his all to God; faith can do no more and God demands no more. When we come to our wits' end, and cry to the Lord in our trouble. He brings us out of our distresses and makes the storm a calm. Then we are glad because we are quiet and are brought to our desired haven (Psalm 107:27-30).

Here am I

This is the second time that Abraham answers thus (v. 1). Without doubt this is intended by God to teach us the true attitude of faith. Abraham displayed ready and willing obedience. He did not drag his feet in following God. His obedience was instant and unquestioning.

The ear that is turned to God obediently when the command is grievous will ultimately hear the command of God that brings all joy. Often there are believers who wonder how they may know the will of God. We believe that ninety per cent of the knowing of the will of God consists in willingness to do it before it is known. When we are ready to pick up the knife or to lay it down, God will pour out His richest blessings.

Verse 12: Now I know that thou fearest God

The omniscient God knew from eternity what the outcome

202

of this test would be, but now there was the full triumph of faith in the life of Abraham, and that would stand before all generations as an example of the utmost in faithful obedience. The knowledge which God had was now shared with Abraham, and this, in itself, would further increase the growth and development of the patriarch.

Faith may be timid when it has not been fully tested, and although we are never to trust in previous triumphs but in God alone, those triumphs are there as landmarks of the trustworthiness of God.

Thou hast not withheld thy son

Abraham certainly did not offer up his only son to God because he thought that God was a monster who would punish him if he did not obey. He offered up his son because he was able to persuade Isaac to join in the full surrender to the faithful and unchangeable God, assured that Isaac would be restored to life even though he was reduced to ashes, and that in him all promises would be fulfilled.

Verse 13: Behold behind him a ram caught in a thicket

It is doubtful whether Abraham understood what substitution was to be made when he answered Isaac's inquiry by saying that God would provide Himself a lamb. The principle of substitution is here enunciated in the Biblical development of the doctrine of the Saviourhood of Christ. With each story of sacrifice — Abel, Noah, Abraham — there is revealed a little more knowledge of vicarious, substitutionary atonement. In Isaiah 53 is the first revelation that the lamb is to be a man. John the Baptist points out and identifies Christ as the Lamb (John 1:29). God was instilling a reflex in the minds of His people so that every time they thought of sin they would think of death, for sin means death. It means the death of the sinner or the death of the Saviour.

Verse 14: Abraham called the name of that place Jehovah-Jireh

There is scarcely a geographical name in Palestine that does not call attention to the mercies of God. At places of remarkable deliverance or extraordinary blessing the children of God erected a memorial or gave it a name that posterity might recognize the goodness and grace of God. Abraham named the place "The Lord will provide," and in that very place God provided His Lamb as Abraham unwittingly prophesied. The meaning of this text is that the Lord will intervene for His people in the hour of their necessity.

It is said to this day

This action of the Lord passed into a proverb which exists in multitudes of languages. "The Lord will provide" is a proverb which God established to show all His creatures that He is the same at all times for all His people and that the fountainhead of His provision is the cross of the Lord Jesus Christ.

In the mount of the Lord it shall be seen

It should be translated, "In the mount the Lord shall be seen." The idea is that God will always intervene for His people in the hour of their need. He may not come at the time or in the way that our impatience may desire.

"The Mount of the Lord" is Calvary. There is no blessing that does not come to us by the way of the cross. There is the fountainhead of all grace. God's covenant of grace is as much in force today as at any moment of history, and if we go to the mount of the Lord we shall be blessed, for nothing can stop the blessing that flows from Calvary.

Verse 15: The angel of the Lord called

To one who has manifested triumphant faith all the cohorts of heaven will come to instruct, to bless and to manifest further the glories of God. The greatest trial recorded of any believer (for who else has ever been commanded to sacrifice his own son?) became the occasion of wonderful revelation. Heaven pronounces blessing upon the child of faith. The triumph of faith becomes the background of a proverb that declares the Lord's continuing faithfulness to all His people.

Thus all believers are taught that the Lord will interpose for them in the hour of necessity. His messenger confirms the promises and binds God by a mighty oath to perform wonders on behalf of the trusting soul.

Out of heaven the second time

The angel spoke first to arrest the sacrifice of Isaac. The

204

second time he spoke to announce blessing upon blessing in unending flow because the Lord had been honored by magnificent faith. The action of Abraham was causing God to bear a wonderful testimony in his behalf. God will not require you to offer up an only son, but indeed the equivalent is required of every believer: is he not directly commanded to "hate his own father and mother and wife and children and brothers and sisters, yes, and even his own life," in comparison with Christ (Luke 14:26, RSV)?

There is no difference between persons or times; the same applies to all His followers, in every age and place. On no lower terms will any human being be acknowledged as a friend of Christ; nor will any child of man who is unwilling to comply with them find acceptance with Him in the day of judgment. If the angel is to pronounce blessing, we must die on the altar with Him.

Verse 16: By myself have I sworn

Abraham's action had caused God to speak from heaven, and renew His promise to Abraham, and, for his more abundant consolation, to confirm it with an oath. The New Testament enlarges upon this, saying that "since he had no one greater by whom to swear, he swore by himself . . . So when God desired to show more convincingly to the heirs of the promise the unchangeable character of his purpose, he interposed with an oath, so that through two unchangeable things . . . we . . . might have strong encouragement" (Hebrews 6:13-18, RSV). This, God tells us, is an anchor for the hope of our souls, we being the heirs spoken of here.

Because thou hast done this

Nothing in man merits the grace of God; the promises of God are entirely free and result wholly from His sovereign grace. God frequently manifests His love toward us in consequence of something that we alone have done.

We must remember that Abraham was once an idolator and that God had appeared to him alone (Isaiah 51:2), and made these promises to him while he was still in Ur of the Chaldees. But now, because Abraham has shown the most remarkable faith of any man in history, God renews these same promises, and binds Himself by an oath, swearing by Himself, so that we who are to inherit these promises may have a stronger basis for our faith. The faith of Abraham brings forth an amazing oath and promise, while we in no wise lose our reward if we give even a cup of cold water in His name (Mark 9:41).

Verse 17: I will bless thee

The key to this promise is the word "offspring." It is not the posterity of Abraham, but of the Lord Jesus Christ. It is specifically noted in the New Testament, "It does not say, 'And to offspring' referring to many; but, referring to one, 'And to your offspring' which is Christ" (Galatians 3:16, RSV). This multiplication of promise, then, refers to the Lord Jesus, and we understand its infinite magnitude, only when we comprehend that He is the source of measureless grace.

I will multiply thy seed as the stars of the heaven, and as the sand which is upon the seashore

The multiplication of Christ in individuals who came out of the loins of Abraham will be stupendous. The church — that body of people called to Him between the day of Pentecost and the day of His return — will be with Him in glory.

Abraham will have a posterity that will fill heaven like the stars, but will also fill earth like the sand. Here is one of a long series of texts which leads me to believe that when our earth has passed away, and all the elements have melted with fervent heat (II Peter 3:10), there will be "a new earth in which righteousness dwells" (II Peter 3:13). This earth will be filled with a perfect human population — far superior to Adam — and this population will be the children of Abraham.

And thy seed shall possess the gate of his enemies

The offspring is Christ (Galatians 3:16), and He possesses the gates of His enemies. By His death upon the cross, He laid the foundation for sin to be abolished. In His death, He abolished death forever (II Timothy 1:10). As the risen Lord, he said to John, "Fear not, I am the first and the last, and the living one; I died, and behold I am alive for evermore and I have the keys of Death and Hades" (Revelation 1:18, RSV). On the cross He despoiled the powers of Satan, made a show of them openly, and triumphed (Colossians 2:15).

206

Verse 18: In thy seed shall all the nations of the earth be blessed

The ultimate fulfillment of the text will not take place until that glorious time when the earth is full of the knowledge of the Lord as the waters cover the sea (Isaiah 11:9). But even today there is a visible fulfillment before our eyes. We here in this western world are blessed because Christ died. In the seed of Abraham, all the promises became available even to us, Gentiles, who once were not a people. The nations today are cursed, and our presence as the salt of the earth, keeps the mass from utter decay. But when Christ comes again, Israel will be restored, and then there will be "life from the dead" for the nations (Romans 11:15).

Verse 18: Because thou hast obeyed my voice

God comes back to this again and again. In this chapter, Abraham is recorded as having performed the most extraordinary act of obedience that ever was known from the foundation of the world. His great act of faith called forth from God the confirmation of the promise, strengthened by oath, and guaranteeing all blessings to Abraham.

The importance of obedience cannot be overestimated. When we obey God without question we confess that we are finite and that He is infinite. We acknowledge that He has all knowledge and that we have no wisdom. We show, by our obedience, that we believe He is good; that His plans are best for us; that He is full of grace and lovingkindness; that, in every way, He is wonderful, good, wise, and loving.

Verse 19: Abraham returned unto his young men

He had announced to the young men that he and Isaac would return (22:5). And now the two came down the hill together. On that return journey there was the holy and reverent joy that was none the less overflowing and abounding. This return of the father and the son gives us a glimpse of the infinite joy in the hearts of the heavenly Father and the Lord Jesus Christ on the day of the resurrection.

There is no mention in the Bible of the joy in the Godhead at the resurrection of Christ. We read of Christ's joy in dying, but the greater joy is veiled by a silence which cries out that it is impossible to tell the joy of heaven in the language of earth. An ocean cannot be put into a cup.

207

They rose up and went together

Abraham was going down the hill to sorrow and death, but his vision was filled with heavenly things and nothing, henceforward, would be recorded of him except quiet triumph through the daily round of life. The days of lingering on the road from Ur were over. The days of sidetrips to Egypt and Gerar were past. The past of Abraham, the justified one, was as a shining light and it would glow most brightly at evening. The men who had waited at the foot of the mountain would live with Abraham in peace and plenty, even as the world today is blessed because of the presence of believers. We walk together as the light of the world and the salt of the earth.

Verse 20: Milcah she hath also borne children

The paragraph about Abraham's distant family is introduced at this point in the narrative to illustrate blessing and fruitfulness that comes because of faithfulness to God. Christ was the promised offspring in whom all the nations should be blessed. All creation would be blessed because of Isaac's sacrifice. Palestine is called the Holy Land, not because it is a better land, but because there a hole was dug to hold the cross of Jesus Christ. His offering is to be felt beyond Jordan and to the uttermost parts of the earth.

The promise is that many afar off shall be blessed in Him. Abraham believed God, and blessing began in his own family before going to all the families of the earth. Obedience to God brings rich blessing even to the natural things of life. " . . . because you hearken to these ordinances, and keep and do them . . . there shall not be male or female barren among you, or among your cattle" (Deuteronomy 7:12, 14, RSV). This is our heritage as believers and fellow-heirs with Abraham of the blessings of God.